Hart,
Thanks for y[...]
dedication of Harvest 2000, you
play such a big part in keeping
that vision alive in our hearts.
Together, we will reap a harvest.
Our God is faithful.
                    Merry Christmas!
                    NGCF-1998
                    I Tim. 1:12

The Basics of Life

4HIM

The Basics of Life

Walking on the Side of Faith

Andy Chrisman
Kirk Sullivan
Mark Harris
Marty Magehee

HOWARD
PUBLISHING CO.

THE ARTISTS DEVOTIONAL SERIES

Our purpose at Howard Publishing is to:

- *Increase faith* in the hearts of growing Christians
- *Inspire holiness* in the lives of believers
- *Instill hope* in the hearts of struggling people
  everywhere

  Because He's coming again!

The Basics of Life
© 1998 by Andy Chrisman, Kirk Sullivan, Mark Harris, Marty Magehee
All rights reserved. Printed in the United States of America

Published by Howard Publishing Co., Inc.,
3117 North 7th Street, West Monroe, Louisiana 71291-2227

98 99 00 01 02 03 04 05 06 07   10 9 8 7 6 5 4 3 2 1

Library of Congress Cataloging-in-Publication Data
The basics of life : walking on the side of faith / 4HIM.
      p.   cm. — (The artists devotional series)
   ISBN 1-878990-85-3 (hardcover)
   1. Meditations.   I. 4HIM (Musical group) II. Series.
BV4801.B27 1998
242—dc21   98-12445
                                                    CIP
Interior design by LinDee Loveland
Manuscript editing by Philis Boultinghouse

Scripture quotations are from the Contemporary English Version *(CEV)* © 1995, American Bible Society. Used by permission. Scriptures marked NIV are from the New International Version, © 1973, 1978, 1984 by International Bible Society. Used by permission Zondervan Bible Publishers.

Dedicated to

our wives,

our families,

our children,

to those who make sacrifices

while we're on the road,

and most of all,

to Him

American Bible Society
1-888-505-7500

We hope you enjoy this book, but more importantly, we hope you enjoy the Book, the Bible, that inspired the songs and devotions contained in this book. We are proud to use the Contemporary English Version of the Bible throughout this book and hope you enjoy getting to know this translation.

The Bible is the foundation of our Christian life and also the foundation of 4HIM. That is why we feel so strongly about our involvement with the American Bible Society. They exist for one reason: to put the Word of God into the hands of every person on this planet.

Since 1993, 4HIM has partnered with the American Bible Society, sharing the need for Bible and Scripture distribution. We have had tremendous success, but still the need is great. Opportunities abound for anyone who wants to share in our efforts with ABS. Your involvement could change someone's eternity. If you feel led to help, simply call the toll-free number above and do what God lays on your heart.

Join in our thanks to the American Bible Society for caring enough to distribute God's Word around the world.

Blessings,

4HIM

Contents

PART TWO
...a **Love** that is blind

PART THREE
...a **Faith** that is frevently grounded in Christ

Contents

PART FOUR

...a **Hope** that endures for all time

Introduction

What are the basics of life? Do social status and peer acceptance top the list? Or is life all about accomplishments and achievements? Some seek the fame that comes to athletes and music "stars"; others crave adult toys—and they have to be bigger, faster, and better than the ones before. The pursuit of education and knowledge are a high priority for some people, while others seek self-awareness and self-actualization.

But surely life is more than any of these things. Status and toys won't love or comfort us when we feel alone. Money offers no security beyond the grave. What good are fame or education if we lose our families—if we lose our souls? To be truly successful, in both this life and the one beyond, we must focus our hearts on the basic ingredients

1

of life. And that is what we are trying to do in this book. The chorus of "The Basics of Life" sums up what we're trying to say.

> We need to get back to the basics of life
> A heart that is pure
> A love that is blind
> A faith that is fervently grounded in Christ
> The hope that endures for all times
> These are the basics
> We need to get back to the basics of life

A heart that is pure . . . Purity of heart means seeking the things of God; it means keeping ourselves unspotted from the world. It means being open and yielded and eager to learn.

A love that is blind . . . God loves us in spite of the realities he sees in us; his vision is changed by the blood of Jesus that covers us. And this is the kind of love he calls us to offer those around us—a love that looks beyond reality and extends mercy.

A faith that is fervently grounded in Christ . . . Faith in Christ is the link between people and God. Without faith, we have no hope of eternity with him, and without faith we have no grounding to secure us in the inevitable storms of life.

The hope that endures for all time . . . The Christian's hope is not merely "wishful thinking"; it is not just *wanting* something, but *expecting* a certain outcome based on absolutely reliable promises. Our hope gives purpose to this life and secures our future life.

Writing this book has been a new experience for us and one that we have thoroughly enjoyed. Using some of our favorite songs as backdrops, we have explored some of the basic lessons of life that God has taught us in our faith walk. We don't claim to be theological scholars, but we are four guys who have come to know Jesus Christ in very real ways. He makes a difference in every aspect of our lives, and our dependence upon him continues to grow.

It is our prayer that what we have written will draw you closer to God and to his Son, Jesus—if that happens, we will have accomplished our purpose. If you'll keep your eyes focused on the Savior, everything else will fall in line, and you will be securely grounded in the basics of life.

...a **heart**

heart that is pure

I still believe in the old rugged cross

I still believe there is hope for the lost

BASICS OF LIFE

DON KOCH, REED ARVIN AND FRED HAMMOND • EXECUTIVE PRODUCER • AUDWIN

BENSON

84418-2960-2

H I M

PRINTED IN THE U.S.A.

The Basics of Life

Marty Magehee

Our kitchen looked like the aftermath of an active war zone, with crusty pots and pans towering above the sink, traces of flour and sugar lacing the floor, and a thin layer of smoke-like steam rising from the stove. My beautiful wife, Sheri, was poised amid the fray with spatula in hand, looking every bit the part of the fabulous cook she is. For hours she'd been slaving over the line of fire, whipping up all sorts of casseroles, quiches, meat pies, and whatever else she'd found enough ingredients to make. By watching one of those Ala-Martha Stewart daytime programs, she'd discovered a way to prepare a month's supply of our favorite main courses and then store them away for later use. So, whenever the next thirty-one dinner bells would roll around, all she'd have to do is walk from the freezer to

...a heart that is pure

from the album
THE BASICS
OF LIFE

The Basics of Life

We've turned the page, for a new
    day has dawned
We've rearranged what is right
    and what's wrong
Somehow we've drifted so far from
    the truth
That we can't get back home
Where are the virtues that once
    gave us light
Where are the morals that
    governed our lives
Someday we all will awake and
    look back
Just to find what we've lost

(Chorus)
We need to get back to the basics
    of life
A heart that is pure and a love
    that is blind
A faith that is fervently grounded in
    Christ
The hope that endures for all times

the microwave, and *voila!*—
instant home-cooked meals. I
married an amazing woman.

After giving her the night off
and scouring Hamburger Hill, I
started thumbing through her
recipe box to see what she'd been
throwing together. As I scanned
her index cards, I began to pick
up on something that's probably
far from revelationary to a seasoned cook like Sheri, but for a
novice like myself, it was quite a
revelation. Running through
each recipe was a common
thread—salt. It seemed to be the
one basic ingredient that had the
power to make or break the flavor of everything she'd made.
Without salt, her entire day's
work would have wound up
hugging the bottom of a garbage
bag.

In Matthew 5:13, Jesus said
that his followers "are like salt for
everyone on earth"—the one
basic ingredient that has the
power to make or break the destiny of every soul that hungers
for a taste of eternal life. We as
Christians have been commis-

8

sioned to bring savor and hope to an otherwise bland and lifeless creation.

We live in a spiritual ice age, where compromise and individualism have frozen shut every heart refusing to accept the simplicity of following Jesus. Salt substitutes like transcendental meditation and New Age consciousness are constantly being proposed by those who wish to alter an already complete recipe. Some have gone so far as to rule out the very existence of God, setting themselves up as deities. If we are to melt away these chilling deceptions, the salt in our lives must be pure. If even one grain of a worldly salt substitute is introduced into our "salt shakers," we contaminate our witness and become just as guilty of compromise as those we're trying to reach.

In Matthew 16:6, Jesus told his disciples, "Watch out! Guard against the yeast of the Pharisees" because he knew how easily our human nature could feed on their teachings. In reminding us how responsive an entire lump of dough is to even the smallest amount of yeast, Jesus was warning us against the takeover potential of false doctrines. With a dash of materialism here or a pinch of false humility there, we can gradually drift away from the "pure and spotless" motive of James 1:27, without ever noticing the change. This is why Paul said, "We must give our full attention to what we were told, so that we won't drift away" (Hebrews 2:1). He, too, was aware of how easily these tiny granules can creep into our character and effect everything we are.

So, it's probably not a bad idea to practice some salt evaluation every now and then. By asking ourselves questions about why we do and say certain things, we can

...a heart that is pure

These are the basics,
We need to get back to the basics
    of life

The newest rage is to reason it out
Just meditate and you can over
    come every doubt
After all, man is a god, they say
God is no longer alive
But I still believe in the old rugged
    cross
And I still believe there is hope for
    the lost
And I know the rock of all ages
Will stand through the changes of
    time

(Chorus)

(Bridge)
We've let the darkness invade us
    too long
We've got to turn the tide
Oh and we need the passion that
    burned long ago
To come and open our eyes
There's no room for compromise

(Chorus)

get a clearer picture of what
we're adding to the recipe of our
lives:

- Do we give in order to get?
- Do we compliment others
  only because we want to
  be complimented?
- Are we competitive with
  everyday life issues?
- Do we seek revenge at any
  level?
- Do we say or do things in
  an effort repackage our own
  agendas as "God's will"?
- Are we more fascinated
  with the signs and wonders
  that accompany the power
  of our Christian walk than
  we are with our names
  being written in heaven?

These are some of the many
questions I ask myself every
day—and I'm not always
thrilled with the answers. Even
though the truth is sometimes
hard to face, I need to ask the
questions in order to keep a
check on my human weak-
nesses. It's something we all
need to do. None of us are
beyond the yeast of the Phar-

isees. Our salt can become stale and useless, fit only "to be thrown out and walked on."

If the words of Jesus were timely in the days of Matthew, I can't imagine how they must cry from his heart today. We've been given the basic ingredients to complete God's recipe for abundant life; now it's up to us to sift the salt substitutes from the genuine seasoning.

The salt of God's message of grace has the power to melt frozen hearts, heal wounded spirits, and preserve the life of every dying soul. If we remain faithful to the basics, we'll not only affect the world we now live in; but, like Sheri's killer chicken casserole, we'll be one day pulled from the oven and our sweet-smelling savor will fill the halls of heaven.

Questions to Ponder

1. What properties of salt make it so essential to life?
2. Do you see the evidence of any "salt substitutes" creeping into your life, such as materialism, compromise, or individualism? What gives you the most trouble? Why?
3. Whom are you affecting as salt? What power of salt is affecting their lives—preservation, flavor, etc.?

Back to the Basics

Nothing is as basic to the recipe of life as salt. God intended for you to be salt to the world around you. Contemplate your relationships with friends and family members. How are you "salting" their lives? Do you bring flavor and seasoning to their thinking? Do you hold out the hope of preservation? Ask God to help you evaluate the quality of your "saltiness."

11

...a heart that is pure

Lord I am desperate for your handiwork

I'm ready for the change

HE NEVER CHANGES
PUZZLES
WHY?
**WHEN THE WALLS COME DOWN
*CHISEL MEETS THE STONE
*FACE THE NATION
**OVER THE HORIZON
**A MAN YOU WOULD WRITE ABOUT
WHEN I GET HOME

FACE

THE

NATION

BENSON
MUSIC GROUP

C GROUP INC.
e in the U.S.A.

EVERY REASON TO BELIEVE
*TAKE ME TO THE PLACE
WHEN I GET HOME (REPRISE)

Produced by: **Don Koch**
*Produced by: **Chris Harris for Funattic Productions**
Produced by: **Reed Arvin for Casa de Pepe Music
Executive Producer: **Andy Ivey**

> It [ ] fun to be corrected. In fact, at the time it is always painful. But if we learn to obey by being corrected, we will do right and live in peace.
>
> Hebrews 12:11 *CEV*

Chisel Meets the Stone

Andy Chrisman

I was on tour with 4HIM when I got the call that Dad had fallen off the roof of a two-story building. After the initial scare was over and we got Dad into the emergency room, we were relieved to find that nothing was broken that couldn't be repaired. Thankfully, he landed on the only part of his body that wouldn't kill him or confine him to a wheelchair—his rear end. But he was pretty messed up. His pelvis was shattered and several of his vertebrae were broken. He would have to be confined to the hospital for several weeks, but we thanked God for graciously protected him from more serious harm.

As Dad began to heal, we noticed a marked change in his personality. He became much more open with his emotions—he went from handshakes to hugs, from wallflower

13

...a heart that is pure

from the album
FACE THE
NATION

Chisel Meets the Stone

There is a man inside of me who
    wants to have his way
And I cannot comply I relinquish
    this heart of mine
Lord I am desperate for Your handi-
    work I'm ready for the change
And I can't wait to see what You
    can do with me
It was for my joy You endured the
    cross and I am overwhelmed
I want my wheels to turn for You
    not for myself

(Chorus)
Let my eyes be fixed on the hope
    that cannot fail
May my life be set where the
    hammer meets the nail
Place my feet where the rubber
    meets the road
Shape my heart to please Your
    eyes alone

to socialite, from unemotional to charismatic. He was different. He told me that during his stay in the hospital, the song "Chisel Meets the Stone" constantly ran through his mind and that he drove the nurses and x-ray technicians crazy as he made each one of them sit down and listen to him sing every word of the song.

He had always had it in him—this zest for life, this affection for people—but now he was just a little more transparent. It took a traumatic experience to open that curtain to his soul.

I've learned through the years that in order for God to make us into what he wants us to be, we must first be broken into dust. Like a trophy that is knocked off its mantle and shattered into bits, I, too, must sometimes be allowed to fall from my "comfort shelf" and be broken. Such a fall is not my idea of fun—in fact, it hurts. But I know that Christ endured pain for us, and I know he endured that pain so that we would be changed.

The allegories in the chorus of "Chisel" paint some rather painful

pictures—a nail being hammered into place; the screech
and smoke from the friction of a tire hitting the pavement;
a sculptor's chisel striking the rock, chipping away everything that doesn't belong. It takes guts to ask the Lord to
take out his hacksaw and prune our lives to conform to his
vision for us. It takes courage to allow him to stretch us
beyond what's comfortable so that he may achieve his *Loan*
dream for us. But I've come to realize that if I want to be *Trust*
who God wants me to be, pain will be part of the process. *finances*
Only when we have been broken can God's creative *healing*
process truly begin—from the ground up. *relationship*

Is there an addiction, a lust, a craving in your life that's
hard to give up? Is it difficult to turn off the TV and pick
up the Bible? Has resentment or bitterness kept you from
forgiving someone who's hurt you? Whatever it is, it's
time to go under the knife on the operating table of the
Great Physician.

I don't want to have to keep falling off my "comfort
shelf" and being broken to bits in order to have my spiritual attitudes changed; I'd rather allow God's Word to
gently mold me into a godly man. But I don't always
respond to his Word with real change. I guess some truths
are only learned the hard way. It is my prayer that my
heart accepts whatever it takes to make me into the man
God wants me to be.

Pain can be a good thing, believe it or not. Okay, not too
much pain . . . but a little now and then reminds us that
we're still human and that God has not given up sculpting
his masterpiece.

...a heart that is pure

cont.

That I may live my life where the
chisel meets the stone

Fill my mind with images of what
You want of me
The path that I must take lest I lose
my way
For my home is in Your sovereignty
my destiny to be
Faithful before Your face to serve
at the throne of grace
And as evil comes to cloud my
sight and lure me away
I will not be distracted from this
holy place

Chip away what tries to hide the
truth
Until there is a remarkable
resemblance of You

Chisel Meets the Stone by Billy Simon
and Justin Peters © 1990 River Oaks
Music Co./BMI/Locally Owned
Music/BMI/Justin Peters Music/BMI.
River Oaks Music Co./BMI/Locally
Owned Music adm. by Meadowgreen
Group, Nashville, TN. Justin Peters
Music adm. by Justin Peters, Nashville,
TN. International copyright secured. All
rights reserved. Used by permission.

Questions to Ponder

1. Have you ever had a painful experience—physical or emotional—that worked real change in you? What was it?
2. Why must we sometimes be broken in order for God to work his will in his?
3. Is God working in your life right now to stretch you out of your "comfort zone"? What is he trying the change in you? How are you responding?
4. What valuable lessons have you learned from painful experiences?

Back to the Basics

Spend some time today in honest communication with your heavenly "sculptor." Ask him what there is in you that he wants changed. Pray the prayer of Psalm 139:23–24: "Look deep into my heart, God, and find out everything I am thinking. Don't let me follow evil ways, but lead me in the way that time has proven true."

...a heart that is pure

Lord here am I, I will be the one

I'm committed to finish until the setting of the sun

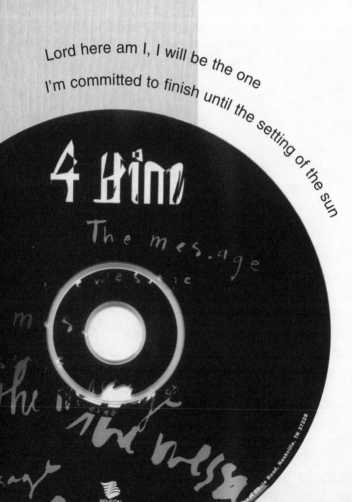

You are like a letter written by Christ and delivered by us.
But you are not written with pen and ink or on tablets
made of stone. You are written in our hearts
by the Spirit of the Living God.

2 Corinthians 3:3 CEV

....

The Message

Mark Harris

*Contract
Covenant*

I signed my first book deal when I was six years old.
Even at that young age, I knew it was the right thing to do.
With innocent, childlike faith and the blessings of my parents, I gave my story rights to the oldest, most established
publisher, editor, and author in the universe.

As with any contract, both parties had certain responsibilities. My responsibility was to relinquish all rights to
the story of my life to the publisher and to give the publisher the authority to add paragraphs, pages, and chap-
ters at will. In return, the publisher agreed to look after all
of my interests, to shape and mold my career as he knew
best, to stick with me as publisher through good times
and bad, and to give me the necessary tools to success-
fully endure the process to its completion. Many people

19

...a heart that is pure

from the album
THE MESSAGE

The Message

The fields are white and now the
    time has come
For there's a harvest, there is work
    left to be done
Lord, here am I, I will be the one
I'm committed to the finish until the
    setting of the sun
Lord, I will be faithful in all I say and
    do

(Chorus)
To live a love that never fails
To love my neighbor as myself
And to give till there is nothing left
    to give
To live a faith that never dies
To be crucified with Christ
Until all that lives through me
Is the message

I can't ignore what's right before
    my eyes

before and after me have signed lifetime deals with this powerful force. Who is this old, established entity? God.

Choosing to give up the rights to our life stories can be a frightening decision. Allowing someone else to add to, delete from, and rearrange our own plans for our lives requires absolute trust. How can we know this God is worthy of such trust? Is it really smart to relinquish control of *everything?* Well, with God, it's everything or nothing at all. When you sign on with him, you sign away your whole life.

And of all those agents vying for control of your life, God is the only one who has *your* interests at heart. Because God is all-powerful, he can take the worst manuscript and turn it into a moving masterpiece, and because he is all-loving, he uses his power in your life only for good. Some of his changes may be painful at the time. You may grimace as he deletes one of your favorite pastimes, and you may groan as he writes in a whole new section on purity and self-control, but the

20

end product will fill you with joy unimaginable and with peace that passes understanding.

And his work in your life is not only for your own benefit. He uses the pages of your life to bless others as well. There are some people in this world whose only impression of God is what they see in you. As they read the pages of your life, they see the heart of God. Saint Francis of Assisi said, "Share the gospel at all times, and if necessary, use words."

The world has *heard* our message for thousands of years, but in this age of skepticism, they must be able to *see* it as well. As we live out the pages of our lives, can they see in us a love that never fails? They have heard the word *love* used and abused, but can they see the reality of love written in the way we, as followers of Christ, live our lives? As we surrender our lives to Christ, "the author and perfecter of our faith" (Hebrews 12:2 NIV), he will write his message of love and hope on our hearts for all to read and believe.

The message written on our hearts is written not with ink but with the Spirit of the living God. The words God writes on our hearts are *alive*. They offer hope to the hopeless, grace to the fallen, mercy to the guilty, and love to the "unlovable." The eyes of the world are looking for a statement of Truth lived out in real life. They are reading the testaments of our lives, hoping against hope to find something real and tangible that they can believe in.

If the stories of our lives are to be worth reading, then we must relinquish all rights to the author and perfecter of our faith and allow him to shape his story in us until all that remains is his message living through us. As I try to meet the requirements of my book deal, I pray I will live my life in such a way that in the end the title of my story

21

...a heart that is pure

For all around this world is searching for a sign
Outside the door they're living in
the night
And the light that lives within me is
the hope
They long to find
So I must be faithful in all I say and
do

(Chorus)

(Bridge)
If we all will work together
We can make this world a better
place to live
We can make a difference if we try

(Chorus)

(Chorus)

Is the message
Is the message

The Message by Mark Harris, Don Koch, and Michael Omartian © 1996 Paragon Music Corp./Point Clear Music/ASCAP/Definitive Music (admin. by Word, Inc.) Dayspring Music (a div. of Word, Inc.)/BMI/Class Reunion Music/Middle C Music/ASCAP. All rights reserved. Used by permission.

will read, "I have fought well. I have finished the race, and I have been faithful" (2 Timothy 4:7).

Questions to Ponder

1. Have you signed your life story over to God? How are you doing in keeping up your end of the bargain?
2. How has God rewritten your life thus far? What purpose can you see in his edits?
3. What areas of your manuscript have you yet to relinquish to God's control? How will you start to let go?
4. Who has God put into your life to read the message written there? What do those readers see?

Back to the Basics

Look back at your basic "contract" with God. Relive the willingness to entrust it all to him that you felt then. Rather than give in to the temptation to "renegotiate" your book deal and take back some of the control, renew your commitment to give it all over to him.

...a heart that is pure

Freedom can only be found in the blood of Jesus

Freedom can only be known in the love of God

BASICS OF LIFE

BENSON

84418-2968-2

H I M

If the Son gives you freedom, you are free!

John 8:36 *CEV*

Freedom

Kirk Sullivan

Freedom. Ask a thousand people what that word means, and you'll get as many answers. Though its definition is elusive, the thirst for its promise is universal. The pages of every history book record stories of countless men and women who have fought and died in pursuit of this priceless commodity.

Even in the short history of our young country, we find a legacy of war—from the Revolutionary and Civil wars, to World War I and II, to the Korean conflict, the war in Vietnam, and the Persian Gulf War. All of these battles were waged in pursuit of freedom. The blood of countless bodies was spilled for the sake of freedom. And by most measures, America has maintained the freedom she has fought for across the centuries. We have freedom of

...a heart that is pure

from the album
THE BASICS
OF LIFE

Freedom

An old man once said when the
   war is over we would be free
He said that we'd have to drive
   those Nazis back to Germany
His vote in the post-war years was
   a steadfast cast for FDR
'Cause he thought that the new
   deal would heal a nation's
   bleeding heart

A man in his middle years shed
   tears about the economy
He said that the balance of the
   deficit would set us free
He was caught in a fragile state
   'cause the Dow had never
   sunk this far
So he searched for the deliverance
   at the bottom of a bottle
   at a local bar

(Channel)
Everybody
Everybody wants to be free
But I'm here to tell you

speech, freedom of choice, and freedom of religion. But are we truly free?

While Americans exercise many outward freedoms, inwardly, we are a country enslaved to chemicals, greed, pornography, and debt. Spiritual bondage has more power to destroy our lives than any political or military enemy of any kind. Several years ago I met an evangelist with a testimony of freedom. Before becoming a Christian, this man was convicted of armed robbery. While serving his prison term, he met a warden who shared his witness with him. As a result, this man gave his life to Christ. He now says that when he accepted Christ, he felt more free than he had ever felt outside the prison walls. Though his body was still confined, his mind and soul were free to soar in his salvation in Christ.

But most of us begin our search for freedom in the wrong places. Before coming to Christ, my friend Jay tried to find freedom by drowning his problems

26

in a bottle—but to his dismay, he discovered that his problems could swim! Many of us play the "if only" game in our search for freedom: If only we could get out of debt, we would be free. If only we could find the right person to marry, then we'd be free to express and fulfill ourselves. Or if only we were no longer married, then we would be free—free to do what we want without hindrances or responsibilities.

But the Bible tells us that the redemption we seek is not purchased "by such things as silver and gold that don't last forever . . . but by the precious blood of Christ, that spotless and innocent lamb" (1 Peter 1:18–19). His blood—the blood of the spotless lamb—is the only blood that can buy our freedom. His blood is the only substance that will remove our guilt and break the yoke of sin. It is in Jesus, and him alone, that we find freedom from the sin that plagues our lives and separates us from our Father in heaven.

So much of our search for freedom is really a search for peace and rest, is it not? And of all the places you've looked for peace, have you ever found it outside of Christ? I thought not. The following sweet words of Jesus soothe even the most jaded ear: "If you are tired from carrying heavy burdens, come to me and I will give you rest. Take the yoke I give you. Put it on your shoulders and learn from me. I am gentle and humble, and you will find rest" (Matthew 11:28–29). Isn't that what you've been looking for all along—rest and peace?

Let's make a commitment today. When we feel bound by walls of worry or stress, when we're weary from trying to shoulder our problems alone, when our lives are filled with unrest and fear, let's run to the Cross of Jesus. Fall at

...a heart that is pure

(Chorus)
Freedom
Can only be found in the blood of
   Jesus
Freedom
Can only be known in the love of
   God
Freedom
Comes to whoever would dare to
   believe Jesus is
Freedom
A child once spoke of the hour
   when school would end and he
   could play
His freedom waited for him at the
   ending of another day
His dream was to get to his home
   for a stickball challenge on the
   avenue
If he could get past the dealer sell-
   ing dope in the middle of the
   hall at the grammar school

(Chorus)

Freedom by Geoff Thurman and Lowell
Alexander © 1992 Meadowgreen Music
Co./ASCAP, Nashville, TN. International
copyright secured. All rights reserved.
Used by permission.

its base and allow his liberating blood to unlock every door. "Freedom comes to whoever would dare to believe."

Questions to Ponder

1. How would you define freedom?
2. What enslaves you or prevents you from experiencing freedom?
3. What wrong places have you looked for freedom, and what have the results been?
4. What does the death of Christ set us free from? How?

Back to the Basics

Freedom has been a basic principle of our country since its foundation, but we often confuse the ability to do what we want with true freedom. Search your heart for spiritual chains. Hold out your shackled wrists to your heavenly Father and ask him to cut the chain and set you free. Ask him to teach you how to use your freedom in his service.

...a heart that is pure

You're the Light of the world I pray that all will see

Only you know the way to put our puzzles in place

HE NEVER CHANGES
PUZZLES
WHY?
**WHEN THE WALLS COME DOWN
*CHISEL MEETS THE STONE
*FACE THE NATION
**OVER THE HORIZON
**A MAN YOU WOULD WRITE ABOUT
WHEN I GET HOME

FACE
THE
NATION

EVERY REASON TO BELIEVE
*TAKE ME TO THE PLACE
WHEN I GET HOME (REPRISE)

Produced by: Don Koch
*Produced by: Chris Harris for Funattic Productions
**Produced by: Reed Arvin for Casa de Pepe Music
Executive Producer: Andy Ivey

Always honor the Lord. Then you will
truly have hope for the future.

Proverbs 23:18 *CEV*

Puzzles

Andy Chrisman

Lucas loves jigsaw puzzles. He and I start a new one together at least once a month. He's only five, and yet he refuses to attempt one smaller than five hundred pieces. Anything easier insults his abilities. And really, the only thing I help him with are the edges. Once his boundaries are set, he's on his own to complete the picture. With the image of the fully assembled puzzle on the box beside him, Lucas is on his way, enthralled for hours at a time.

Life is like a jigsaw puzzle (add your best Forrest Gump impersonation there), except for one big difference—we aren't provided with a snapshot of what our life should look like at the end. We have no way of knowing what our lives will look like five, ten, fifty years from now. But God does. He's the die-caster, creating each piece to fit perfectly

...a heart that is pure

from the album
**FACE THE
NATION**

Puzzles

I remember that first day I heard
  Your voice
I could feel Your quiet peace drown
  away the noise
Your oracle of truth still rings in my
  head
I've come to know my path just as
  You said
And I see the sham the lie that
  swallows the man
People need to see

(Chorus)
It's a dangerous life without Your
  wisdom for our ways
It's a gamble with time when we
  don't hear You when You say
You're the Light of the world I pray
  that all will see
Only You know the way to put our
  puzzles into place

There's a fire dark as night in an
  evil rage
Spreading power to searching
  souls at a deadly wage

into his master plan. And the hard part is already done—God set up the boundaries an eternity ago through his Word. The Bible gives us the moral guidelines for every decision we'll ever have to make. Now it's up to us to make the judgments of which piece goes where.

To get a clearer picture of what the puzzle should look like, we need an idea of what God sees for us during our lifetime. Some of the pieces represent suffering and loss; others are victories or blessings or a job change or marriage. There are good times and hard times; you put this piece here and that piece over there, and they all fit together somehow. Before you know it, you'll start to get a glimpse of who you are and what you're about.

Have you ever lost a puzzle piece? There aren't many things more frustrating than working for weeks on a huge picture and coming up a piece short. Lucas' sister tends to be a disruptive force once we start a puzzle. Bless her heart, she just wants to help. But being two years old makes her the proverbial bull in the china shop when we're trying to finish Darth Vader's head. And that's when the fight starts. My son will protect his masterpiece with his life, and no little gremlin is gonna mess it up.

I can't begin to tell you how often I've let the devil rob me of my joy, my money, my time, my energy—I let him steal vital pieces left and right. And do I put up a fight to protect myself? Not usually. Most of the time, I'm a willing accomplice. And the picture becomes jumbled. I try to force an ill-fitting piece where it doesn't belong, and before long I'm overwhelmed, thinking there's no way I'll be able to finish. I just want to put the whole thing back in the box and forget about it.

But that's when God shows himself to be a good daddy. He reacts to me just like I do to Lucas (in my better moments) when he gets frustrated: "It's all right, son. We'll work together, and we'll get it done." But God can give me something I can't give Lucas—replacement parts. No matter what I've lost, God has an endless supply of duplicate pieces. He's going to make sure that I have the opportunity to see myself as he sees me—perfect and extraordinary. "Look how those pieces came together," he'll say to me one day.

The day I put the final section in will be the day I stand in heaven face to face with my Creator. Until then, I'll keep looking for fractions that fit, trying not to get discouraged by all the pieces that still remain on the table.

...a heart that is pure

I want to scream a plea, a warning
  sign
Take the stutter from my step,
  don't let my tongue be tied
Piece after piece Your love in holy
  relief
Into the picture You have seen

(Chorus)

Light up the shadows
Expose the deception
Reveal the illusion
Unscramble the puzzles people
  need to see

Questions to Ponder

1. Are there any "puzzle" pieces in your life right now that just don't seem to fit? What are they?
2. In what ways have you tried to live your life outside the boundaries God has set up? What was the outcome?
3. As you look at completed sections of your puzzle, what new perspectives do you have on events that "puzzled" you at the time?

Back to the Basics

Step back from the puzzle of your life and take a moment to look at the basics. How has God fulfilled your basic needs for love, acceptance, and security? How has he created order out of chaos? What beautiful sections has he brought together in the puzzle of your life? Take a moment to be thankful for parts of your puzzle that make sense and renew your commitment to trust him to fit all the remaining pieces together.

Broken hearts
~~scribbled out~~

Unfulfilled careers
dreams
finances
health - marriage
friends dying - (Kim)

Tree growing in
water / Pull out
from roots
hole fills in /

You want ever
know their
was A tree -

Protect your masterpiece (heart, soul,
Pleasing God)

...a heart that is pure

But there's a power in my soul greater than us all

And I'm reminded I am not my own

I heard the Lord ask, "Is there anyone I can
send? Will someone go for us?" And
I said, "I'll go. Send me!"

Isaiah 6:8 *CEV*

Voice in the Wilderness

Marty Magehee

The soybean field was cold and obscured by a blanket of early morning mist. Decoys were laid out in their usual random pattern, setting the stage for our last goose hunt of the season. My buddy and I sat pensively, hunkered down inside a rusted-out steel drum that served as a makeshift blind, deeply imbedded within the heart of the main levee.

After waiting out in the frigid air for what seemed like hours, we heard the distant shots ring out like bugle reveilles, calling everyone to arms. It was thirty minutes before sunrise—time for the game to begin.

Four hours later and not a single goose to cook, we packed up every bit of the ammo we'd brought and sulked away like a couple of little leaguers whose play-off game

37

...a heart that is pure

from the album
O B V I O U S

Voice in the Wilderness

I stand among the millions
And I can't help but feel so small
I am just a speck of dust
A particle existing on this great big
    spinning ball
The part of me that's human
It tells me I am not that strong
There's a power in my soul,
Greater than us all, and I'm
    reminded
 I am not my own

(Channel)
I'm yielded to a higher calling
The reservations of my soul are
    falling
Yea, they are falling one by one
    and I am

(Chorus 1)
One voice shining through the dark-
    est night
One voice standing up for what is
    right
One voice, nothing more and
    nothing less
Than a voice, crying out, out in the
    wilderness

had gotten rained out. As we began our trek back across the levee, we heard a familiar sound that dropped us to our knees. Geese—lots of geese. They were honking and gabbling in an adjacent field just over the next rise.

After crawling on our stomachs for a hundred yards or so, we slowly scaled the embankment, guns in hand. As our line of sight broke the top of the levee, neither one of us was prepared for what we saw.

Stretching out for approximately two hundred acres was nothing but a sea of geese. Thousands of them. We lay there motionless, as if we'd been hypnotized. Suddenly, a desperate call from a scout goose pealed out right above our heads and sent the entire gaggling throng into flight.

To describe their reaction as loud and dramatic would be like calling the universe a big place. We dropped our guns, jammed our fingers in our ears, and stared upward at the firmament of feathers that was churning no more than thirty feet overhead.

There we lay, paralyzed with awe long after the last tuft of down drifted to the ground.

It's amazing how the warning signal from one goose could move thousands in an instant. Above the clamor of their mindless chattering, one lonesome cry got through.

What would've happened if this goose had suddenly realized it was no different from the rest of those grazing in the wetlands below? Where would some of these birds have ended up if the appointed sentry discovered he looked just like the rest of them? What if he started thinking that one little sound wouldn't make any difference, anyway, because the chances of the other geese hearing it were slim? My guess—goose gumbo.

We live in a civilized wilderness, and we have been appointed as messengers of warning—scout geese, if you please. Our appointment is not something we can choose to accept or not accept. It is not a suggestion; it is a mandate. Matthew 28:19 says, "Go to the people of all nations and make them my disciples." This command doesn't leave room for inferiority complexes. It requires a reckless surrender to a power and ability much more efficient and capable than our own.

God has equipped us with everything we need to be messengers of warning. If we allow the Holy Spirit to speak through our everyday lives, our voices will cut through any walls of confusion that the enemy erects. If we reject our calling, our fellow "geese" will never notice the evil hunter—lurking, poised, ready to fire on unsuspecting souls.

Like the scout goose, we have been lifted to a higher plane of vision; we are able to see the hunting ground for what it is. It's now left up to us to sound the compassion-

...a heart that is pure

The voices of confusion
Can fill a world that's all my own
Running havoc thru my mind, all the
    truth and all the lies.
It's so hard to sift the right from
    wrong
In the middle of the choosing
Through the clutter of this human
    noise
When my words fall to the ground
All the dust has settled down
All that matters is your still small
    voice

(Channel)

(Chorus 2)
One voice shining through the dark-
    est night
One voice standing up for what is
    right
One voice nothing more and noth-
    ing less
Than a voice, crying out, a voice in
    the wilderness
One voice breaking through the
    silence
One voice given to remind us
One voice, nothing more and
    nothing less
Than a voice crying out, a voice in
    the wilderness

ate warning to everyone with an ear to hear. All that's required of us is simply to say, "I'll go. Send me!"

Voice in the Wilderness by Mark Harris and Marty
Magehee © 1998 New Spring Publishing, Inc./Point
Clear Music/ASCAP (both admin. by Brentwood-
Benson Music Publishing, Inc.)/ASCAP/Word Music
(a div. of WORD MUSIC)/Round Square Music
(admin. by WORD MUSIC)/ASCAP. All rights
reserved. Used by permission.

Questions to Ponder

1. Have you ever been in a situation that called for action and suddenly lost confidence? Think back over that circumstance. What was it that caused you to falter?
2. Where does 2 Corinthians 3: 4–6 say that our confidence comes from? How can believing this Scripture help you to fulfill your appointment as a messenger of warning?
3. What will happen to the non-Christians around us if we don't sound the warning call?
4. What special insight do we have concerning "the hunter" that those in the world do not have? How can we use this insight to help others?

Back to the Basics

If you saw that a friend of yours was about to be hit by a truck, you would instinctively call out a warning. It's a fairly basic human characteristic: when we see someone we care about, or even a perfect stranger, about to be harmed physically, we shout out or rush to their aid. But when it comes to the spiritual, unseen realm we don't always feel the same urgency. Ask God to give you eyes to see the reality of the spiritual warfare that surrounds you.

...a heart that is pure

Baptize me and bury me until only you remain

I don't want to be the man I was before the river came

A   e won't be afraid! Let the earth tremble and
        ntains tumble into the deepest sea. Let the
                ocean roar and foam, and its raging
                waves shake the mountains.

Psalm 46:2–3 *CEV*

Before the
River Came

Mark Harris

Keith Dudley stood on his balcony, staring at the
flooded honky-tonk district below. What had once been a
thriving night spot, filled with bars, clubs, and crack
houses, was now at the bottom of the riverbed. Gone were
the places that only yesterday provided fake shelter for the
thousands who spent their days and nights restlessly
searching for answers in bottles and drugs and other vices.
All that remained were memories of what used to be.

Keith is a friend and co-writer, and he'd been working
on songs for an upcoming album. As he stood, taking in
the destruction below, God sent a revelation: At times, our
lives are very much like the honky-tonk district below the
hotel room Keith was staying in, filled with things that
temporarily satisfy the flesh but ultimately destroy us.

43

...a heart that is pure

from the album
O B V I O U S

Before the River Came

I've been lookin' at the past
I've wasted too much time on
    things that won't last
I've built a kingdom out of rubble
    and sand
But I don't, don't want to hold on
    to it all
I'm ready for the river to run
And wash it away, I'm singin'

(Chorus)
Come sweet water, cleanse my
    soul
Shower me and make me whole
Consume me with Your healing
    flood
Leave no traces of the man that I
    was
Before the river came

There's no freedom in the chains
They'll hold you captive to the guilt
    of your stains

And the Spirit of God is like a raging river, flooding our lives and washing away our sin.

Unlike the patrons and proprietors of the night spot, we have a choice in regard to the flood. The river of God is constantly flowing, looking for those who are willing to be overtaken with all that the river has to offer:

- For those who are diseased and sick, the river offers healing and hope.
- For those filled with lust and perversion, it offers righteousness and purification.
- For those entrapped in fear and worry, the river offers peace.
- For those lost in poverty, it is a river of blessing.
- For those filled with hatred, the river spills over in love.
- For those filled with sorrow or sadness, the river brings joy.
- For those plagued by doubt, it is a river of faith.

44

- For the hopeless, it carries hope.
- For those bound in chains of past and present sin and failure, the river overflows with forgiveness and grace.

We can choose to stand aloof and above the raging river, analyzing its movement and talking about its force, simply observing. Or we can let down the levee of our flesh and allow the river to consume us. The book of Joel says that "in the last days, God will pour his spirit upon all flesh (NIV)." The pouring has begun. The river is rising. Those who stand on the riverbed and allow it to flow over and consume them will be forever changed. Those who stand afar and observe remain dry and unchanged, but even they are only a levee away from transformation.

The cleansing force of the flood wipes our souls clean of all traces of sin and failure. It has the power to cleanse our souls and make us whole. And when we have been consumed, the memory of our past will serve only as a reminder of all that has been washed away, all that we have been delivered from. Invite the river to consume you:

> Baptize and bury me until only you remain.
> I don't want to be the man that I was
> Long before the river came.

...a heart that is pure

One drop of water brings an ocean
   of change
And I long, I long to move on from
   it all
I'm ready for the river to run
And wash it away, I'm singin'

(Chorus)

(Bridge)
Baptize and bury me until only You
   remain (come and rescue me)
I don't want to be the man that I
   was
Long before the river came

(Chorus)

Questions to Ponder

1. What in your life needs to be washed away by God's river?
2. How is it that a force so powerful as a raging flood could bring peace and cleansing to those consumed by it?
3. What aspects of the river (listed on the previous pages) do you long for most?

Back to the Basics

Water is one of the basic elements of our earth. Its power to cleanse and refresh is undisputed, but the fierce force of a flood is not usually something we desire. But imagine being filled and consumed by the river of God. His forces will do us no harm; though powerful and overwhelming, they refresh and cleanse. Take a step of faith into that riverbed. Stand fast as the river floods over and through you. Surrender to the force of the flood.

...a heart that is pure

Oh to have that kind of faith and love

What a solid man of faith God was

HE NEVER CHANGES
PUZZLES
WHY?
**WHEN THE WALLS COME DOWN
*CHISEL MEETS THE STONE
*FACE THE NATION
**OVER THE HORIZON
**A MAN YOU WOULD WRITE ABOUT
WHEN I GET HOME

FACE
THE
NATION

GROUP INC.
the U.S.A.

BENSON
MUSIC GROUP

EVERY REASON TO BELIEVE
*TAKE ME TO THE PLACE
WHEN I GET HOME (REPRISE)

Produced by: Don Koch
Produced by: Chris Harris for Funattic Productions
*Produced by: Reed Arvin for Casa de Pepe Music
Executive Producer: Andy Ivey

> Let love and loyalty always show like a necklace,
> and write them in your mind. God and people
> will like you and consider you a success.
>
> Proverbs 3:3–4 *CEV*

A Man You Would Write About

Marty Magehee

Everyone wants to be remembered. Whether it's for something we've accomplished or for profound words we have spoken, we all dream of being eulogized in some way. The human spirit longs to have an effect beyond the grave. This isn't a bad thing. As a matter of fact, this quality is designed and imparted by God to every creature made in his image. Put quite simply: it is the character of God to desire praise.

I shared several college classes with a guy who desperately wanted to be praised as a pastor someday—but not just any pastor. He envisioned himself as a legend for God. And by all human standards, he had what it took to ride his dream into reality. He was sharp, good-looking, extremely focused, hardworking, and dedicated to God

...a heart that is pure

FACE THE
NATION

A Man
You Would
Write About

From the time time began
You always chose a man
To lead the people safely by Your
way
To be a voice and echo what
You say

Like David or Abraham
Your word is full of such men
And if the Bible had no closing
page
And still was being written to this
day

(Chorus)
I want to be a man that you would
write about
Oh a thousand years from now
That they could read about
Your servant of choice in whom
You found favor

and people. He learned all the right lines and perfected his delivery, honing his niche for a future in sharing the gospel.

But as he approached his senior year, I began to notice a peculiar mutation creeping into his personality. His voice and entire demeanor started to change. In fact, every time I talked with him, even in passing, I felt as if he were orating to me from behind some imaginary pulpit. He became more interested in church politics than praying with us in the dorm chapel. After graduation, he continued his pursuit of grandeur until the numbers game consumed his concept of ministry and he began to lose touch with those closest to him. We've since lost contact, but my hope is that God is currently writing a new chapter in his life that proves to be more favorable than what I've just written.

This classmate of mine is no different from me or anyone else who seeks praise from the wrong source. When we seek praise from our fellow creatures rather than from the Creator of all, we pervert our God-given desire for *his* praise into a desire for the acclamation of men. What God intended as a way of drawing us closer to his heart gets somehow twisted into self-absorbed pride. We take a heavenly longing, perfect in innocence, and taint it by bringing it down to an earthly level. Sometimes we even deceive ourselves by claiming to seek praise from our creator, when in reality we seek applause from his creatures.

God's formula for being the kind of man and woman he would write about begins with his pointed instructions in the book of Proverbs: "Let love and faithfulness never leave you; bind them around your neck, write them on the tablet of your heart. Then you will win favor and a good name in the sight of God and man" (Proverbs 3:3–4 NIV). Love and faithfulness are merely the starting points for a much larger outline involving subtopics that reach into every area of our lives. We'll never achieve the noteworthiness we desire until each one of these ingredients are in their proper places and growing for God's purposes—not ours.

The guy I knew in college sought recognition and great-ness, but the greatness he sought was self-serving and shallow. I know someone else who, although he did not seek recognition, has taught me all I need to know about greatness. His background was meager, and his early death ugly; but the magnitude of his life in between was too wonderful to be contained in the pages of this world. He was always the servant, putting everyone else's needs before his own. He dearly loved his father and never stepped outside the parameters of his instruction. When-ever he did anything sensational, he shied away from the inevitable sensationalism that followed. Nothing clever or

...a heart that is pure

A man who heard Your voice
Generations away
It is my prayer that they will look
   back and say
"Oh to have that kind of faith and
   love
What a solid man of God he was"

(Chorus)

highly marketed ever fascinated him. His only dream was to complete God's will for his life, keeping love and faithfulness ever before him. As a result, God lifted this young man, Jesus, to the heights of heaven and has written his name on the heart of every believer—he's a man you would write about.

Questions to Ponder

1. What would you like to be remembered for?
2. When is it good to desire praise?
3. How does this holy desire for praise get distorted?
4. What does Proverbs 3:3–4 say will win us favor and a good name? How are you pursuing these qualities?

Back to the Basics

Focus today on living and thinking in ways that will bring approval from God. Be on your guard against efforts to gain praise from the people around you.

...a heart that is pure

You sent love to live in us, so we just need
To trust the signs and wonders of the heart

I am you Creator, and before you were born, I chose
you to speak for me to the nations.

Jeremiah 1:5 *CEV*

Signs and Wonders

Andy Chrisman

I'm not the kind of person who lets many people in. I
don't throw open the doors of my heart and yell, "Hey,
y'all! Come on in. It's a party in here!" I'm about as private
as you can get.

For months, Dana Cappillino thought I hated him. As
the new guitarist in Truth, Dana set out to win over his
new colleagues. He knew it was important to test the
waters with each of the twenty-five or so of us who lived
on the forty-foot bus. And wouldn't you know that the
first person he approached was me. I didn't give him
much encouragement. After giving only courtesy answers
to his "Where ya' from?" and "How long have you been
on the road?" my nose went right back into whatever book
I was reading.

...a heart that is pure

from the album
O B V I O U S

Signs and Wonders

We don't need a psychic line to tell
us what is on Your mind
We don't need to search for
what is hidden in the stars
We don't need a horoscope to
bring us life to give us hope
You are God so we just need to
trust who You are

You sent love to live in us
So we just need to trust the signs
and wonders of the heart

(Chorus)
You light the dark
You are
Truth in love
So we just need to trust the signs
and wonders of the heart

We don't need a clever scheme,
political positioning
We don't need a guru on the outside looking in

As time went by, I began to get
somewhat of a reputation for
being unfriendly. That label
really hurt. That was not who I
wanted to be. I began to question
my identity. Should I change?
Should I try to be the life of the
party? I needed some advice. So I
went to my wife, she being a
social butterfly, and asked her to
teach me how to be more outgoing.

Now, I've got to tell you something about Jackie—besides
being a butterfly, she's a wise
woman, wise beyond her years—
and she gave me some sound
advice: "God made you this way
for a purpose," she told me.
"Don't try to be something
you're not." While she told me
that a 180 degree personality turn
was not necessary, I could
smooth out some of my rough
edges and work a bit on my people skills.

All of us want to know who
we are and if who we are is okay.
That's why so many people pay
$3.99 a minute to talk to a "psy-
chic" to learn about their futures
or why they religiously read their

horoscope—they want to know who they are and where they're going. But God did not put the answer to those questions in the stars. We know who we are because we know who made us—and we have been made in his image. And we may not know what our future holds, but we know the one who holds our future.

Over the years, I've found comfort in knowing that God knows me completely, whether other people know me or not. God knew me before I was born (Jeremiah 1:5), and he checks up on me constantly (Romans 8:27). I can trust him because he's the one who built me. He understands how I think, what makes me mad, and what floats my boat.

I've also found comfort in Jackie's words that God made me the way he did on purpose—with my aversion to small talk and all. And learning to accept myself as God made me has been incredibly liberating.

And I've learned to open up a little more to people I don't know. And Dana Cappillino and I are now lifetime friends. Even though I've learned to be more open than I once was, I'll never be the open book some people are. But now I understand that I don't need to try to be someone I'm not. I'm just as God made me—unique, unlike anyone else I've ever met. I don't fit into any personality category; I'm not predictable; and the answers to who I am and why I'm here surely don't lie in the alignment of the stars. I am exactly what God desires me to be—me!

...a heart that is pure

We don't need an alibi to justify our
place in life
You are in control, the means will
justify the end

You sent love to live in us
So we just need to trust the signs
and wonders of the heart

(Chorus)

Signs and Wonders by Mark Harris and
Andy Chrisman © 1998 New Spring Pub-
lishing, Inc./Point Clear Music /
ASCAP/New Spring Publishing,
Inc./Andrew Hope Music/ASCAP. All
rights admin. by Brentwood-Benson
Music Publishing, Inc. All rights reserved.
Used by permission.

Questions to Ponder

1. What kind of person are you? Are you open, reserved, somewhere in between?
2. Are you content with the basic personality God gave you? (I'm not talking about negative characteristics, but basic personality.)
3. How can God use your unique personality traits for his glory? Especially think about some of the traits you may not like.

Back to the Basics

Basic personality traits are things like being outgoing or reserved, analytical or spontaneous, orderly or carefree. God uses every personality type to bring about his purpose here on earth. While all of us need to "smooth out our rough edges," God made us the way we are on purpose. Today, as you spend time with the one who made you, ask him to help you see his purpose for you; ask him to liberate you from the desire to be something you're not.

PART TWO

...a **love**
that is blind

I still believe there is hope for the lost

I know the rock of all ages will stand

> For now there are faith, hope, and love. But
> of these three, the greatest is love.
>
> 1 Corinthians 13:13 *CEV*

The Basics of Life

Kirk Sullivan

Things get so mixed up sometimes. Wrong becomes right and right becomes wrong . . . or so it seems. How does our thinking get so twisted?

I was channel surfing one evening when a CNN report caught my attention. The reporter told of an old, historical tree in California that was maliciously cut down by vandals. If the perpetrators were convicted, he said, they would have to pay a hefty fine and possibly serve some prison time. The very next report was about a group of pro-life activists who were protesting outside a Mississippi abortion clinic. The protesters were being cuffed and taken to jail. Conspicuously missing was any discussion on the morality of what was going on behind the closed doors of the clinic.

...a love that is blind

from the album
THE BASICS
OF LIFE

The Basics of Life

We've turned the page, for a new
day has dawned
We've rearranged what is right
and what's wrong
Some how we've drifted so far
from the truth
That we can't get back home
Where are the virtues that once
gave us light
Where are the morals that
governed our lives
Someday we all will awake and
look back
Just to find what we've lost

(Chorus)
We need to get back to the basics
of life
With a heart that is pure and a love
that is blind
A faith that is fervently grounded in
Christ
The hope that endures for all times

How do people's values get so mixed up? How have we become so desensitized to the atrocities in our society? How did we get to the point in our country that cutting down a tree is a serious, "newsworthy" crime while killing innocent, unborn children is not even an issue of discussion?

The answers to our country's demise are twisted and complex, but the road back to godly principles is straight and simple—it's a road paved with the basics of life.

As the song says, we need to get back to the basics of life— back to "a *heart* that is pure, a *love* that is blind, a *faith* that is fervently grounded in Christ, and the *hope* that endures for all time." Sound too simple? These concepts may sound simple, but they are far from simple to live out in our lives.

What does it mean to have a pure heart? I love the Random House Dictionary definition of *pure:* "Without any discordant quality; clear and true." That's the kind of heart God wants us to have. He wants us to have a heart that is not "discordant" with his—one that sings in harmony with his. A heart in harmony with God is submissive and open to his will; it answers his call freely and immediately without any dissenting objections. The definition also said, *clear* and *true*. The quality of our hearts is to ring clear and true when called upon to sing out for him in yielded living. And our hearts can sing for God with clarity and truth only if our devotion to him is wholehearted and undivided. A pure heart is basic to our relationship with God.

What if we lived out a love that is blind—a love that is unconditional, no strings attached? What if we followed Jesus' commandment to love one another as we love ourselves? Our world would be changed in a very basic way. This kind of love would extend to unborn children as well as to those we live with everyday. The way we treat each other—especially in front of nonbelievers—speaks volumes. Our Christianity must surely include prayer, daily Bible reading, and going to church, but it must also be so much more. Our Christianity must be lived out in the way we react to everyday situations, to our spouses, to our children, and to our co-workers. Jesus said that people would know we are his disciples by the love we show one another (John 13:35). Loving each other as Jesus loved us means putting the needs of others before our own, it means forgiving wrongs done against us, it means returning good for evil, it means letting go of the petty differences that keep us apart. These are the basics of life.

How about living a faith that is fervently grounded in Christ? When Christ is the focus of our faith, the inevitable storms that come into our lives will not pull us from our anchor. They may rattle us a bit, we may sway under the force of the winds, but our faith will not be uprooted. If

63

...a love that is blind

These are the basics,
We need to get back to the basics of life

The newest rage is to reason it out
Just meditate and you can over come every doubt
After all, man is a god,
They say God is no longer alive
But I still believe in the old rugged cross
I still believe there is hope for the lost
I know the rock of all ages will stand
Through the changes of time

(Chorus)

(Bridge)
We've let the darkness invade us too long
We've got to turn the tide
Oh and we need the passion that burned long ago
To come and open our lives
There's no room for compromise

(Chorus)

you lose your job tomorrow, will your faith sustain you? If your best friends pull you toward activities you know are wrong, will you remain fervently grounded in Christ? If your health is suddenly taken from you, will you blame God or will you seek his guidance in faith? These are the basics of life. God did not promise us a life without problems, but he did promise us that he would never leave us and that he would always sustain us. Our faith is basic to life.

And what of the basic ingredient of life that we call hope? Hope has the amazing ability to transport our minds from a current crisis to a future joy. Hope helps us lift our eyes off the broken pieces in front of us to see the big picture of God working in our lives. Hope gives the man with a debilitating disease the ability to keep trying. Hope allows the wife whose husband just left her to believe in a future life of fulfillment. Hope allows the college student who has just failed a major exam to see a way to work things out. Hope carries us through those times of despair by helping us see the future God has in store for us. Hope is a basic of life "that endures for all time."

When we get our minds focused on the basics of life, we see that in reality wrong is still wrong and right is still right and God is still in control. The simple basics of life—love, faith, and hope—are really all we need. We can't undo all the world's wrongs, but we can affect the corner of the world we live in if we'll just stick to the basics—the basics of life.

Questions to Ponder

1. What things might "pollute" our hearts and affect their purity?
2. What's the difference in conditional love and unconditional love? Is conditional love truly love?
3. What trying circumstance has your faith brought you through? How did your faith make a difference in your attitude and behavior?
4. How is the hope that God offers different from hoping you'll do good on a test or hoping your house deal goes through?

Back to the Basics

What about the four qualities discussed here qualifies them as basics of life? Meditate today on these four qualities. Examine your life to see how they are growing in you. Ask God to fan into flame the small sparks of faith, hope, love, and purity of heart that already exist in you until they are a fervent flame that brings glory to him.

...a love that is blind

I'm not one to second guess what angels have to say

But this is such a strange way to save the world

CHRISTMAS
The Season of Love

...CED BY: Don Koch EXECUTIVE PRODUCER: Andy Ivey

...on Of Love

6 Do You Hear What
I Hear

7 In Your Care

...own Of
... It Came
Midnight Clear
A Manger
Night!
Night!

10 A Strange Way To
Save The World

BENSON
MUSIC GROUP

COMPACT
DISC
DIGITAL AUDIO

4HIM

> But God chose the foolish things of this world to put
> the wise to shame. He chose the weak things of this
> world to put the powerful to shame.

1 Corinthians 1:27 CEV

A Strange Way to
Save the World

Mark Harris

He was your average Joe—a nice, conservative young man, part of the blue-collar work force of a small town. He had a pretty, young girlfriend, whom he planned to marry. Both lived simple, uneventful, low-key lives, until one day when a visit from a stranger changed everything.

Pregnant! How could she be pregnant? Joe had known Mary for quite some time. How could his virgin girlfriend be pregnant? This new development would destroy their reputations. Poor Joe.

But the pregnancy was not all Joe had to deal with. He and Mary had been visited separately by an angel, and Mary was claiming that the baby she carried was the Messiah and that the Holy Spirit was the father. Talk about more than the average guy can handle! Joe must have

...a love that is blind

from the album
THE SEASON
OF LOVE

A Strange Way to Save the World

I'm sure he must have been
    surprised
At where this road had taken him
'Cause never in a million lives
Would he have dreamed of
    Bethlehem

(Channel)
And standing at the manger
He saw with his own eyes
The message from the angel come
    to life
And Joseph said

(Chorus)
Why me. I'm just a simple man of
    trade
Why Him with all the rulers in the
    world
Why here inside this stable filled
    with hay

thought about running away and leaving Mary alone to sort things out on her own—let *her* explain this to the town folk. He hadn't asked for this responsibility. No one had given him any choice in the matter.

You and I have never had this same experience, but we do know what it's like to feel overwhelmed by circumstances beyond our control. Everything is as it should be, flowing along smoothly, nothing but the expected, tolerable, things coming our way. Then all of a sudden, *wham!* we're called on to do far more than we feel capable of, more than we are comfortable with, more than we want to do.

Sometimes God takes us out of our comfort zone so he can stretch us and perform his will in and through us. God takes ordinary people in ordinary situations and does extraordinary things. That's what he did with Joseph.

Certainly, Joseph's plan for his life was different from God's. He was a simple carpenter who would someday have a family with his childhood sweetheart, Mary. They would raise the kids, then move to the outskirts of Nazareth to a retirement cabin on the Jordan—reputation intact. However, this new twist of events would change all those plans and would require some careful navigation.

Why me? Joseph must have thought. Why not choose a king, priest, lawyer, doctor, movie star, or some other well-to-do Jew to be the earthly father of the Messiah?

But God knew why, because God knew Joseph. He knew he could trust Joseph; this was the role he had created Joseph to play. He put the fiber and character in Joseph required to be father to the Son of God. Even so, Joseph was not forced to accept this mantle; he could have chosen a different road. He could have abandoned Mary and the baby. He could have built a strong case to justify walking away; after all, this wasn't even his child.

Like Joseph, we all have choices to make, each and every day of our lives. And sometimes we are required to make *major* choices. Sometimes, we come to a fork in the road of life, and we have to *choose.* And it all comes down to "God's path" or "my path." God's path is the road less traveled. It may take us to a Gethsemane or a Calvary. "Our path" usually takes us to the Hawaiis or the Caribbean cruises of life.

It's not that God is against us having fun. But God wants to grow us, to shape and mold our character. He knows what's best for us. He knows what will bring us the most joy and the most fulfillment in the end. Extraordinary things through ordinary people—that's God's way. He takes a carpenter and uses him to help fulfill his promise to save the world.

...a love that is blind

Why her she's just an ordinary girl
Now I'm not one to second guess
What angels have to say
But this is such a strange way to
  save the world

To think of how it could have been
If Jesus had come as He deserved
There would have been no
  Bethlehem
No lowly shepherds at His birth

(Channel)
But Joseph knew the reason love
  had to reach so far
And as he held the Saviour in his
  arms
He must have thought

(Chorus)

Now I'm not one to second guess
What angels have to say
But this is such a strange way to
  save the world
Such a strange way, this is such a
  strange way
A strange way to save the world
A strange way to save the world

Maybe you feel useless to God, ordinary, and incapable of anything magnificent. But God created every fiber of your being. He has a purpose and plan for your life. Just as he trusted Joseph to do the work he had created him to do, he trusts you in the same way. The question is, Will you trust him to use your ordinary life to do extraordinary things?

While you're thinking it over, just remember: God uses strange ways to save the world.

Questions to Ponder

1. Have you ever felt overwhelmed by circumstances beyond your control? What were the circumstances?
2. While in the middle of the difficult time, did it occur to you that perhaps God was working a purpose you were unaware of? As you look back on that period of time, can you see God's hand? In what ways?
3. What extraordinary things has God worked in your life thus far—things that were beyond your own ability?

Back to the Basics

When you get right down to it—down to the basics—we really have nothing except what God has given us. As we grow in this understanding, we grow in our contentment with who he has made us to be. Make a commitment today to surrender all you are into his hands so that he can work his purpose in you.

...a love that is blind

It's more than a fable or an old fairy tale

It's the greatest, greatest story ever told

4 Him

The message

BENSON

365 Great Circle Road, Nashville, TN 37228

The Scriptures say, "Humans wither like grass, and
their glory fades like wild flowers. Grass dries up,
and flowers fall to the ground. But what the
Lord has said will stand forever."

1 Peter 1:24–25 CEV

Greatest Story
Every Told

Mark Harris

The first song I ever learned, my dad taught me when I
was four years old:

> For God so loved the world
> He gave his only son to die on Calvary,
> From sin to set me free.
> Some day he's coming back,
> What glory that will be.
> How wonderful his love to me.

Our family attended church every Sunday, and I had
the privilege of singing that song many times for our small
church.

As a child, via the flannel graph, I learned about all the
biblical characters from Adam to John the Revelator. And

...a love that is blind

from the album
THE MESSAGE

Greatest Story Ever Told

When I was a child I heard a great
   story
Of kingdoms and empires and
   prophets of old
Of heroes and martyrs who died
   for their cause
And through every chapter the
   story was told
Of redemption and love sometimes
   written in red
Headed right to the heart of every
   woman and man

(Chorus)
And down through the ages again
   and again
It's the greatest story ever told
Straight from the pages from the
   beginning to end
It's the greatest story ever told
Wisemen could never begin to
   explain
The measure of grace this
   wondrous book holds

in my childish mind, these men
and women seemed like fairytale characters, far removed from
my life and totally irrelevant. As
I grew a little older, I began to
realize that the stories were true,
but the Bible became no more
personal—it was like the history
books I studied in school.

In high school and college, I
heard speakers refer to the Bible
as the "road map to life" or "life's
instruction manual," and so the
Bible became more than fairytale,
more than history; it became a
book of practical wisdom that
could actually be applied to my
life. From Proverbs to the Sermon
on the Mount to Paul's letters to
the churches, I found instruction
and guidance for my life.

But several years ago, my
view of the Bible changed in a
dramatic way. Suddenly, I saw
the Bible as the living, breathing
Word of God. The Hebrew writer
says, "What God has said isn't
only alive and active! It is
sharper than any double-edged
sword. His word can cut through
our spirits and souls and through
our joints and marrow, until it

discovers the desires and thoughts of our hearts" (Hebrews 4:12).

God means for his word to get under my skin, to cut my heart wide open, to slice into my very soul. The Bible is no fairytale, no history book, not even merely an instruction manual—God's Word is *alive*. The story told in the Bible is ongoing. It is the story of my life, of yours. The little song I sang as a four-year-old child is profoundly alive today, for "whoever" is *me!* My name is written in the pages of the Bible: "For God so loved _Mark_ that he gave his one and only Son, that if _Mark_ believes in him, _Mark_ shall not perish but have eternal life." Your name is there too. Just fill in the blank.

And the story of the Bible unfolds more every day, with new names added daily, hourly, even by the minute. We're all a part of the story. The kind of character we become is up to each one of us. And long after our lives have passed, this book will still be speaking, people will still be making choices, and the author will still be adding to the story.

The other day, I began teaching my son, Matthew, the same song my dad taught me all those years ago. I hope he'll learn much sooner than I did that his name is in that story and song.

...a love that is blind

It's more than a fable or an old fairy
   tale
It's the greatest, greatest story
   every told.

For thousands of years, this pearl
   of great wisdom
Has weathered through changes
   and lasted through years
Many a doubter has risen and
   fallen
The story has never once
   abandoned its course
For the author still speaks to the
   listening ones
Through the voices of men and
   through the pages, the pages of
   love.

(Chorus)

(Bridge)
This world that we live in could
   never contain
The wealth of compassion this
   wondrous book holds
It's more than a fable or an old fairy
   tale
It's the greatest, greatest story
   ever told

Greatest Story Ever Told by Mark Harris
and Brent Bourgeois © 1996 Paragon
Music Corp./Point Clear Music/
ASCAP/WBM Music/SESAC (on behalf
of itself and ADC Music/SESAC). All
rights reserved. Used by permission.

Questions to Ponder

1. How do you view the
   Bible? Fairy tale, history
   book, or living sword?
2. Has the Bible ever cut
   you like a "double-edged
   sword"? Has it "cut through
   your spirit and soul"? Has it
   judged the "desires and
   thoughts" of your heart
   (Hebrews 4:12). Where and
   how did it touch you? How
   did you respond?
3. What role are you playing
   in God's ongoing story?

Back to the Basics

It's never too late to begin a new
chapter in your story. God is
eager to put your name in the
pages of his promises. If your
story is headed in the wrong
direction or if the plot of your life
has taken a sour turn, take your
life to God and ask him to change
your story. He can, you know. All
he needs from you is a blank
page and a willing heart.

...a love that is blind.

You'll be in My care, safely harbored there

My heavenly host will follow you close

CHRISTMAS

The Season of Love

...ED BY: Don Koch   EXECUTIVE PRODUCER: Andy Ivey

...n Of Love

...vas

6 Do You Hear What
   I Hear

7 In Your Care

8 ...d On
   ...tma...

9 ...Rest...
   ...tleme...

10 ...Strange... ...y To
   Save The W...l...

...wn Of
   ...It Came
...idnight Clear
...Manger
...ight!
...Night!

BENSON
MUSIC GROUP

COMPACT
disc
DIGITAL AUDIO

...le Road, Nashville, TN 37228

HIM

Bad news won't bother them; they have
decided to trust the Lord.

Psalm 112:7 *CEV*

....

In Your Care

Andy Chrisman

If I could have one wish, it would be that my children would never leave my sight. I hear stories every day of accidents and abductions. And when I think of the pain the parents of those unfortunate children must go through ... well, it's something I pray I'll never have to experience. If I could just keep them within arm's length, I could protect them from all the dangerous elements around them.

If it were possible for me to be with them every second of every day, watching their every move, giving them advice at every turn, picking them up every time they fall down—how would they feel about my ever-watchful presence? Not too good, I'm afraid. No one wants to be smothered. No little boy wants his dad to kiss his boo-boo in front of his friends. No teenage girl wants her father riding

79

...a love that is blind

from the album
THE SEASON
OF LOVE

In Your Care

Sleep Mary sleep I will be there
    soon
Entering earth through your
    precious womb
My child Oh My mother of earth
Give Me the gift of birth
Sleep Joseph sleep may you
    dream of love
And peace to the earth through
    your newborn Son
Oh raise Me with honor and pride
I will stand by your side

(Chorus)
And I'll be in your care
Safely harbored there
My heavenly host will follow Me
    close
But always remember, please be
    aware
I will be in your care
Now Israel oh my chosen one
The prophets foretold that this day
    would come
I pray you will know I'm your King
Salvation is what I bring

in the backseat on the way to the prom. But, still, it's impossible for me not to want to know where my kids are and what they're doing all the time. How can I find a happy medium, a place where they and I are satisfied with the level of my involvement in their lives?

I left my parents' sight one disastrous night in 1971. As they were watching one of my older brothers play baseball, I was playing with some friends on the other side of the parking lot. My mom and dad's uneventful evening became a nightmare when they saw me lying in the dirt lot, seemingly lifeless, the victim of a near fatal accident. Who knows how many times I had been told to watch for oncoming cars? But it only took one split second of thinking like an excited child, ready to play, to put me in grave danger. I spent weeks recovering in the hospital.

To this day, my mom is still affected by that accident. She can't talk about it without crying. And I was affected too. I bear significant scars—not only physical scars from the surgery, but emotional scars as well. I worry too much about my children's safety, and I constantly drill into their little minds the dangers of running blindly into the street. And I panic every time they step off the curb.

I wonder how God must have felt when he allowed Jesus to step off the curb of heaven into a wild and reckless world destined to run him down. All of the swerving, out-of-control, drunk drivers were out on the streets the night God's son journeyed nearly lifeless up that dusty road. But God looked beyond the immediate danger to a greater good.

Now why on earth would I want to send my children out unprotected into that same dangerous freeway? Because I, too, try to look beyond the immediate danger to a greater good. If I were to continuously impose my will upon them, they'd never learn to discern God's voice on their own. Besides, they're in good hands, better hands, in fact, than mine. Proverbs 3:25 says "don't be afraid of sudden disasters" and Psalm 112:7 promises that a righteous man will not have to fret over the thought of impending doom. Since I can't think of anything worse than losing my kids, those verses give me a measure of peace concerning Lucas and Kayleigh.

As Christian adults, we should also take heart in knowing that we, too, are always under God's watchful eye, never more than an arm's length from the one who protects us with his life. We'll be amazed one day to discover how many times our heavenly Father has shielded us from catastrophe and we never even knew it.

I am in his care. Ultimately, my children are in his care. Anyone who calls Him "Father" is in his care. Is there any better place to be?

...a love that is blind

(Chorus)

(Bridge)
Care for Me and shelter Me in
  childhood
Knowing that someday I'll have to
  go
And though it may seem hopeless,
When I'm hanging on the tree
You can know for certain I'll return
But until then oh, oh

(Chorus)

You'll be in My care
Safely harbored there
My heavenly host will follow you
  close
But always remember, please be
  aware
You will be in My care
You'll be in My care
You will be, you'll be in, you'll be in
  My care
Yes, you will, you will be
You will be, you'll be in, you'll be in
  My care

In Your Care by Mark Harris and Billy
Simon © Paragon Music Corp./Point
Clear Music/ASCAP/Careers-BMG
Music Publishing, Inc./Sparrow Song (A
Div. of The Sparrow Corp.)/BMI. All
rights reserved. Used by permission.

Questions to Ponder

1. What is your greatest fear?
2. How can knowing that God is always watching over us calm our fears?
3. What blessings sometimes come from facing our fears?
4. In the event that something bad does happen to us or to someone we love, will we blame God or turn to him for comfort and strength?

Back to the Basics

Fear is a basic instinct of life; but the anecdote for fear is *trust*—not trust that things will always turn out like we want them to, but trust that God is ultimately in control and that he walks with us through the fire. Fortify your trust in God so you will be ready when disaster strikes by reading the following Scriptures: Psalm 56:3; Psalm 56:11; Isaiah 12:2; John 14:1; Psalm 9:10; Psalm 13:5.

...a love that is blind –

Love is free to grow where heaven's healing waters flow

4 Him

The message

BENSON
MUSIC GROUP

> God Most High . . . have mercy. In the shadow
> of your wings, I ask protection till
> the danger dies down.
>
> Psalm 57:1 *CEV*

Land of Mercy

Kirk Sullivan

The Bible is rich in stories of heroic men and women of faith—people like Moses and Esther, Ruth and Abraham, Jacob and Deborah. Reading the stories of their lives and how God used them inspires us to live and serve God better. But as I read about the great men and women of God and all the wondrous things God accomplished through them, I see that the Bible also records their human frailties—their weaknesses and their sins.

But of all the biblical characters, I identify with David the most—he's my main man! David's life was filled with glorious mountaintop experiences. As a young shepherd boy, he courageously faced the giant, Goliath, and killed him with a sling shot and a single stone. When he grew to manhood, there was no one like him in battle. It seemed

...a love that is blind

from the album
THE MESSAGE

Land of Mercy

This is a strange familiar place
Where I am living
The world that was and what's
  become are not the same
I see the evidence of grace
Without forgetting
How far I've had to come to get me
  where I am today

If justice had the only say
Well I would not be here
Cause less than anything is more
  than I deserve
But I can put the past away
For I've discovered
There's nothing left to judge,
  forgiveness is the final word

(Chorus)
Everywhere I turn I see compassion
  but I'm learning
I'm just a fallen man
In the land of mercy
Love is free to grow where

there was no enemy he could not defeat: "The Lord helped David, and he and his soldiers always won their battles" (1 Samuel 18:14).

But the Bible does not tell us only of David's successes; it tells us of his failures. We learn that our hero got another man's wife pregnant and then had her husband murdered so he could take her as his own. We see the tormented conflict between himself and his son; we see marital unhappiness. Our hero was far from perfect. But it encourages me that God shows us these imperfections. In allowing us to see that a man like David—"a man after his own heart" (1 Samuel 13:14 NIV)—could fall so far and still find forgiveness, God holds out hope that that same mercy is available for you and me.

The most important quality I learn from David is honesty. When David's life got messed up—and it seemed to get messed up often—he confessed his sin openly and begged for mercy (Psalm 6:1–4). Instead of running away from God, like most of us do, he ran straight into the merciful arms of his Father.

If not for God's mercy, David would have been destroyed. I need God's mercy just as much as David did. I don't know about you, but I find myself in a constant struggle to subdue my flesh and make it submit to the spirit of God—just like David. The older I get, the more I realize just how weak and wretched I really am. I'm more aware each day that without the Holy Spirit in my life I would succumb to sin over and over. My only hope is in his mercy and grace. Psalm 136 says over and over that his mercy endures forever!

God's mercy is longsuffering and patient. If I thought God was mad at me every time I failed, I'd be afraid to come to him and ask for forgiveness. I'd have a hard time approaching God and asking for strength to avoid sin in the future because I'd be too worried about my last sin. When we sin, God doesn't disown us; rather he eagerly awaits our return. He *wants* to extend mercy to us; we have only to ask and it is ours.

Don't let Satan defeat you with discouragement over your past failures. Rather, gain joy from the fact that God has brought you out of your past life and has ushered you into the land of mercy. David's secret was confession and communication. God's throne room is always open; his mercy ever available. You, too, can walk with David in the land of mercy.

...a love that is blind

Heaven's healing waters flow
Though I may not understand
I'm living in the land of mercy

It seems I never have to ask
For what I'm given
I see the answer long before I see
the need
No longer looking to the past
As just a prison
For what has been helps me
remember what I used to be

(Chorus)

(Bridge)
Though I may walk through the
valley below
I will not fear because I know who
rules this world
I'm walking through

Love is free
I'm living in the land of mercy
Tell me what you see
I'm living in the land of mercy

Questions to Ponder

1. Who is your favorite Bible character? Why? What strengths and weaknesses did that person have in her or his life?
2. Why do you think God allowed the men who wrote the Bible to reveal the weaknesses of his "heroes"?
3. Why is God so willing to extend mercy to us when we are so weak and sinful?
4. Are there any past failures in your life that Satan taunts you with? What victory do you have over Satan?

Back to the Basics

Sin and failure is as basic to our world as air and water. Ever since Adam and Eve sinned in the Garden, we have been taunted and tempted by Satan. But even on that day in the Garden, God ushered in a plan of mercy and salvation. Bring your sin and failures to God, confess your wrong, and allow his and mercy to heal you.

...a love that is blind

And where the lion walks I will not be afraid

My feet may touch the earth, but my heart is swept away

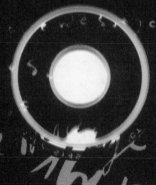

4 Him

The message

BENSON

Live under the protection of God Most High and stay
in the shadow of God All-Powerful. Then you will say
to the Lord, "You are my fortress, my place of
safety; you are my God, and I trust you."

Psalm 91:1–2 CEV

Sacred Hideaway

Marty Magehee

I grew up in a sheltered environment. We weren't
exactly the Cleavers, but there were a few frightening sim-
ilarities. You wouldn't call us "rich," but we always had
plenty of what we needed, and I can't remember my parents ever allowing a crisis to rock our home. Not that they
created a surreal commune environment for my sister and
me, but they didn't give in to the fears of this life. Though
we lived and breathed in the lion's realm, the heart of who
we really were in Jesus gave us perfect sanctuary. I felt safe
and secure in my parents' fearless faith.

But the older I got, the more I took that covering for
granted. I guess you could say I was spiritually spoiled
rotten. I expected God to protect me from all harm. So
when trouble entered my life, I didn't know how to handle

...a love that is blind

from the album
THE MESSAGE

Sacred Hideaway

There's a shadow I can't see
From a holy canopy
That my Father spread for me
When I'm strong or when I'm weak
When I wake or when I sleep
He is watching over me
Over me . . . over me

To the temporary mind
I can't logically define
This love cover so divine
Just beneath what lies between
What is real and what is seen
There is a refuge in His wing
In His wing . . . in His wing

(There's a shadow, I can't see
From my Father's holy canopy
When I wake or when I sleep
He's watching over me)

(Chorus)
I have found a secret place
Where I can go to hide away
Safe inside this hallowed space

it. As a matter of fact, I didn't handle it. I just ran. I got caught up in a cycle of denial, and as a result, I started spiraling deeper and deeper into the problems I wouldn't face. I had heard testimonies from the pulpit of men and women who had fallen from utopia to hell, but until now, I had never considered the possibility that I could get pulled into the fall.

This was the beginning of a very strange time for me. Certain highly dysfunctional ways of thinking began to creep into my spirit. To the enemy, I was like a T-bone steak propped on a pole in the middle of the Serengeti at feeding time. When the least bit of pain and suffering struck, I took that as a sign that God had pulled his hand off of my life. I believed that he had either allowed enemy artillery to reduce his "Holy Canopy" to a shredded joke or that he had simply yanked back the covers of preservation completely. In my mind I created an imaginary stage of hellish backdrops and heckling ghouls. Because I no longer sensed God's protection and didn't understand why he had "deserted" me, I reasoned that some unknown sin had caused a fickle, angry God to leave me shivering and naked on this devilish stage where he brought an end to my life—and all for "the cause of Christ." Now, that's distorted!

And sadly, as I travel, I see this distorted thinking among Christians just about everywhere I go. Many have the twisted perception that God protects his children from all harm—they fail to understand the true nature of God's preservation. What I've finally begun to understand is that sometimes God shows his love for us by sustaining us through hardship, not protecting us from it. Sometimes his plan is not to take me *out* of the wilderness, but to reveal the *oasis* he is growing within me. It was only when I realized his loving intentions for me that I began to release my fears and wild ideas.

While there have been times when God has allowed me to "walk on water" and even "parted the sea" for me on occasion, I know that substantial growth does not come when life is easy and safe. It is only when I find myself in the lion's den that I begin to exercise my faith in his refuge. If my whole life was lived in a sheltered habitat, I would never come to know his power to render my enemies silent and ineffective. If our lives were lived without ever experiencing any form of tribulation—that would be a tragedy.

Many Christians today have yet to see the hand of the Redeemer at work in their storms. As soon as the winds kick up and the bow of their ships begin to rise and fall, they conclude that God's covering has been removed. They assume that if God were on the scene, he would com-

...a love that is blind

I am concealed by saving grace
Forever in this sacred hideaway

Flaming arrows deep in flight
People dropping left and right
Still I'm safely out of sight
Darkness trying to prevail
Demons fighting tooth and nail
But I'm kept within the veil
In the veil . . . in the veil

(There's a place that lies between
What is real and what is seen
A shadow I can't see
When I'm underneath His wing)

(Chorus)

Forever in this sacred hideaway

(Bridge)
Still within this life
There's so much to learn
Barriers to cross
Their bridges to be burned
And where the lion walks
I will not be afraid
My feet may touch the earth
But my heart is swept away
In this hideaway

(Chorus)

Sacred Hideaway by Marty Magehee © 1996
Word Music (a div. of Word, Inc.)/Round
Square Music (admin. by Word, Inc.)/ASCAP.
All rights reserved. Used by permission.

pletely calm their storm. But sometimes Jesus' "peace be still" is not directed at the storms raging outside our lives but at the hurricane whirling within. Sometimes he may want us to trust him to use his covering as a sail to catch the winds and guide us through the waves. God's preservation can come in many forms.

There was a period in my life when I keenly understood that my only hope was God's divine protection. For seven months I was consumed by the darkest, most sinister physical pains I'd ever known. During that time, God's awesome shadow took on the form of illogical peace. It's that same peace that now guides me through situations that, had I not learned to embrace them, would have devastated me and my new family.

As we continue to live where the lion roams, we must learn not to fear his occasional roarings. For without them, we'll never know God's quiet leading or his saving grace that is ever at work, continually sweeping our hearts into his sacred hideaway.

Questions to Ponder

1. In the past, how have you viewed God as your protector?
2. What are some current situations in your life where you are expecting God's preservation to protect you from harm rather than guide you through it safely?
3. Have you ever experienced a pain that God did not remove, yet you felt his presence and love with you in the pain? What did you learn from that experience?
4. What fears still hinder you from trusting God's preservation completely?

Back to the Basics

Self-preservation is a basic characteristic of humans. When harm threatens, we want safety and protection. But sometimes God does not remove the harm; sometimes he allows us to experience the pain. The next time you feel a storm brewing, entrust your life to the one who rules the universe. Ask him to remove the storm, but if he chooses not to, ask him to walk with you every step of the way. Hold tightly to his hand and trust his love to preserve you till the end.

...a love that is blind

We can't deny when the Lord was crucified
He displayed the very meaning of love

The Nature of Love

Kirk Sullivan

Growing up, I didn't have a little brother to pester me,
so when I became an adult, God gave me Andy Chrisman!
And since Andy is the youngest of three boys, he has had
plenty experience in the vocation of pestering. Besides
developing the fine art of pestering as a boy, Andy was
also very active in sports. So now, when 4HIM travels and
the TV is on, Andy is in control of the remote, and you can
be sure he'll be watching some sports event.

One afternoon on the bus during baseball season, Andy
was absorbed in a Ranger's game. I, on the other hand,
was being spiritual. I was meditating and reading Scripture. I'd been thinking about mercy and grace and about
how God deals with sin and disobedience in our lives. My
thoughts were temporarily distracted by the game on TV,

97

...a love that is blind

from the album
THE RIDE

The Nature of Love

Everybody wants to know for
   certain
That love will never leave them
   alone
And there are those who spend a
   lifetime searchin'
For a Juliet or Romeo
Well, I've discovered that one way
   or another
Love will find a way to your heart
It's never too far away or never too
   far apart

There's no mountain too high
There's no ocean too wide
It'll reach beyond the limits
That's the nature of love
Through the measure of time
It'll go through the fire
It is endless that's the nature
That's the nature of love

Some will say that it's too old
   fashioned

and as I watched, it began to
dawn on me that some people
see God as a divine baseball
player, gripping his cosmic
Louisville Slugger, ready to
smack them over the fence whenever they mess up. They see
themselves as a tattered baseball
and God as a fierce batter who
belts them into oblivion every
time they sin.

But as I continued to meditate,
I was reminded that even though
God hates sin, he loves sinners.
One of my favorite Bible stories is
the parable of the prodigal son.
This story pictures God waiting
and watching for us—after we've
totally blown it—with open
arms, ready to restore and forgive. God's intent is not to
destroy us but to destroy the sin
that binds us.

God demonstrated his loving
nature through the ultimate act
of love—sending his own Son to
die in our place. And he did this
while we were still sinners!

> Christ died for us at a
> time when we were
> helpless and sinful. No

one is really willing to die for an honest person, though someone might be willing to die for a truly good person. But God showed how much he loved us by having Christ die for us, even though we were sinful. (Romans 5:6–8)

In my own struggle with my flesh, I am amazed at how lovingly God deals with me when I sin. When I come to him confessing my sin and asking for forgiveness, he doesn't turn me away or beat me down. Rather, like the father of the prodigal son, he runs to meet me. He embraces me and puts the signet ring on my hand and a robe on my shoulders, and he invites all my friends to come to a celebration party in honor of my return!

If you are struggling with sin and worried that God is just waiting to slam you into left field, read again the story of the prodigal son (Luke 15). See the picture of the loving father and imagine him running, with open arms, ready to embrace and carry you home. Jesus is able to deliver you from your bondage; he is eager to restore you to a right standing with God—to make you as if you had never sinned. He desires for you to come to him; he longs to forgive you and fill you with peace. He will withhold nothing good from you, for that is his nature—the nature of love.

...a love that is blind

That love is just a thing of the past
But I believe that only true
   compassion remains
When nothing else will last
We can't deny when the Lord was
   crucified
He displayed the very meaning of
   love
You're never out of His reach
You're never too out of touch

The Nature of Love by Steve Camp, Mark Harris and Michael Omartian © 1994 Word Music (a div. of WORD, INC)/Paragon Music Corp./Point Clear Music/Edward Grant, Inc./Middle C Music/ASCAP. All rights reserved. Used by permission.

Questions to Ponder

1. What distorted views of God do you have?
2. What is the difference in "hating sin" and "hating the sinner"?
3. What is keeping you from running into the arms of your waiting Father? What are you afraid of?

Back to the Basics

Do a little visualization exercise with me for a moment. Imagine yourself, wearily walking down a dusty road, in worn and tattered clothes—defeated because of some sin that drove you away from home. Then lift up your eyes and see at the end of the road your heavenly Father, arms outstretched, running to meet you. Imagine yourself running toward him as fast as you can go; see yourself falling into his arms; feel the warmth and the relief of his forgiving love. Because his nature is love, he will take you back no matter how far you've gone or how long you've been away.

...a love that is blind

Though I have never heard God's audible reply

I hear Him speak unspoken words of life

BASICS OF LIFE

DON KOCH, REED ARVIN AND FRED HAMMOND • EXECUTIVE PRODUCER: WAYNE

BENSON

84418-2960-2

H I M

PRINTED IN THE U.S.A.

The people of this world cannot accept the Spirit,
because they don't see or don't know him.
But you know the Spirit, who is with you
and will keep on living in you.

John 14:17 *CEV*

The Voice of God

Marty Magehee

Many things move me. I guess you could call me a hopeless romantic. Throw a panoramic scene of nature in front of me, and I am spellbound—every time. I've never met a sunset I didn't like. The quiet sway in a Kansas wheat field at dusk or any mountain that even remotely breaks the horizon has yet to leave me uninspired. Whenever I get the chance to sit at the water's edge of a moonlit sea, without fail, I'm overcome with an other-worldly sense of awe that falls nothing short of divine. Everything that human ability can't make speaks to me in a deeply profound way, a way that I can only attribute to the voice of God.

Every one of us has experienced such encounters, but not everyone is willing to hear within them the inaudible

103

...a love that is blind

from the album
THE BASICS
OF LIFE

The Voice of God

I have dreams of being Moses
Standing on the mountain top
When he heard the voice of God
And I admit that even sometimes
I've imagined I was Paul
On the road to Damascus
When he heard the Saviour's call.

(Channel)
But though I have never heard
God's audible reply
I hear Him speak unspoken words
of life

(Chorus)
I hear His voice
Every time I hear a newborn baby
cry
When I hear a sparrow singing at
The dawn of morning light
I hear His voice

heavenly dialogue. I'm amazed whenever I hear Christians say that God doesn't speak to us today. In their refusal to hear, they allow humanism to crack its whip of denial and they stifle the shouts of a creation that orchestrates resounding praises to an invisible God. Unless they see his lips move and hear him speak clearly, audibly, and in a language they can readily understand, they refuse to believe.

Even the simple creatures that roam God's earth portray an obvious awareness of his voice. The baby sea turtle cracks open its shell, bursts through a thick ceiling of sand, and makes a mad dash for the safety of the ocean without breaking stride. A newborn calf strains on its wobbly legs in successful pursuit of its mother's milk. Small birds and insects build nests that rival the methods of modern architecture.

How do these unreasoning animals that we call inferior know the hows and whens to do these things? What points them in the right direction? Is it not God's voice speaking throughout creation every second of every day that keeps all his creation in perfect order? And yet, the majority of God's highest order of creation continues to turn a deaf ear and explain away any link to his leading.

As for me, there is no debate. My very existence is held together by a flow of silent words that are spoken to me daily from the heart of a loving God. The rush I experience from something as simple as a sudden swirl of colored leaves, or the sound of aspen rustling on a Colorado mountainside doesn't stem from a global shift in the tides. When the love of my beautiful wife or the baby blue eyes of my little boy wilt every fiber of my being, the element of chance is not a factor.

God's whisper is deafening. His lyrics stretch far beyond the natural splendor that rises from the earth before me. He steals my attention with a glimpse of his beauty and then blows me away with his unimaginable peace. Without a doubt, "I know I have heard the voice of God."

...a love that is blind

When I hear the thunder echo
 through the sky
When I hear the wind come
 whistlin' through
A forest full of pines
Then I know, yes I know
 I have heard the voice of God.

In this faithless generation
Some refuse to just believe
In a God they cannot see
But I have had a revelation
And I'm as sure as I can be
That the God of all creation
Came to live inside of me

(Channel)

(Chorus)

Questions to Ponder:

1. What in God's creation moves you?
2. What message is God's creation speaking to us?
3. What does it mean to "hear" an inaudible voice?

Back to the Basics

What could be more basic than nature? Spend some time today listening to God as he speaks through his creation. Take a walk; sit in your backyard. Thank God for the beauty of his creation. Take time to hear his voice.

...a **faith**
*that is fervently
grounded in Christ*

I long to know the mysteries of why and who we are

Of what has been and what's in store

My heart tells me to pray. I am

eager to see your face.

Psalm 27:8 *CEV*

The Hand of God

Mark Harris

Neil Armstrong, in 1969, was the first man in history to place his feet on the surface of the moon. "One small step for man, one giant leap for mankind." At last we had reached beyond the limitations of earth and had landed on a surface beyond earth. Driven by the search for life forms other than our own, we since have sent various spacecrafts into the solar system, longing for clues to what lies beyond.

Have you ever wondered why we spend millions on space programs trying to see what might be out there? It seems to me that we are not just searching for other life forms but that we are, in fact, searching for ourselves? Who are we? Why are we here? What existed before us? What lies beyond us?

..a faith that is fervently grounded in Christ

from the album
O B V I O U S

The Hand
of God

I cry for hope, I long for peace
To fill the void of reason that my
    heart can only see
There is a pull, there is a need

I see in part, I search for more
I long to know the mysteries of
    why and who we are
Of what has been and what's in
    store

(Chorus)
But the hand of God is all that we
    are seeking
It burns within my soul to know
    what lies beyond
In the hand of God, constantly it
    reaches
To take us to the place, the place
    we all belong

We all are made of flesh and bone
At times we are so fragile and at
    times we can be strong
But through it all we carry on

The answers to all our questions lie in one place—in the hand of God. If we want to know *who we are*, we need only look to his hand for the answer. The Bible says that we are created in the very image of God. We are his most prized possession, fashioned by his hands while still in our mother's womb (Psalm 139:13). God spared no effort when he formed us; he took care of every detail. He crafted our personalities and talents and implanted in each one of us a blueprint outlining all our future potential.

If we want to know *why we are here*, we find that the answer once again is in the hand of God. Our purpose on earth is to glorify God, in body and spirit, in all that we do. The apostle Paul says that "we were also chosen . . . in order that we, who were the first to hope in Christ, might be for the praise of his glory" (Ephesians 1:11–12 NIV). When we submit our lives to Christ, we fulfill our purpose by living in such a way that others will praise and glorify him.

What came before us? Why God, of course. From his hand we were created out of nothing. From his hand, he created our world and all its creatures. Our history is God. *What lies ahead of us?* I know you're ahead of me on this one—the answer lies in the hand of God. Our future is all arranged. Jesus told us so when he left this earth: "There are many rooms in my Father's house. . . . I am going there to prepare a place for each of you. After I have done this, I will come back and take you with me. Then we will be together" (John 14:2–3). Our future is all taken care of! The questions that have filled the minds of men and women since the beginning of time are easily answered for those who know where to look.

God built within each one of us a desire to reach beyond ourselves to Someone greater than ourselves. He put within each of us a need that is filled only by him. It's as if a huge magnet is pulling at something within us, and we are all searching for the source of that pull. But long before any of us began our quest for that source, he initiated a quest for us.

Ever since the Fall in the Garden, men and women have searched for a way to mend their broken relationship with their Creator, and even then, in the Garden, God initiated a way back to him. The plan for Jesus was set in motion the very day Adam and Eve fell. And when the time was right, he sent his most precious possession, his own Son, to this planet earth to search for searching souls and reunite them with their Creator for eternity. Jesus' crucified, outstretched hands say to all who will hear, "I'm what you are searching for. I am the way to what your heart desires. I'm reaching out to you; I draw you to myself."

...a faith that is fervently grounded in Christ

(Chorus)
For the hand of God is all that we
    are seeking
It burns within our soul to know
    what lies beyond
In the hand of God constantly it
    reaches
To take us to the place, the place
    we all belong

(Bridge)
We are destined from the day that
    we are born
To yearn for something more

(Chorus)

The place we all belong

How I long to know what lies
    beyond
Everybody longs to know
What lies beyond

In the hand of God

All around you, people are reaching and searching for God, trying to find the answers to their most basic questions, trying to find the reason for the pull they feel for Someone more. Though many do not realize that God is the one who is pulling them, we do; and we can be the link that restores fellowship between the two. Drug abusers, homosexuals, alcoholics, atheists, agnostics, prostitutes, adulterers—all are searching for the force that pulls at their hearts. And the answer to all our questions and all our needs lies in the hand that shaped the mountains and hung the stars, the very hand that formed our bodies—the hand of God.

Questions to Ponder

1. Have you ever felt the pull of God on your heart? How did you respond?
2. Can you think of any questions whose answers do not lie in the hand of God? What are they?
3. Are you living your life in a way that fulfills your purpose to glorify God? What needs to change?
4. Is your relationship with God such that you can look forward to your future with peace?

Back to the Basics

The questions we've discussed in this reading are really some of the most basic questions of all. Bring any unanswered or haunting questions right to the throne of God and with the confidence of a loved child, ask your Father to help you understand.

...a faith that is fervently grounded in Christ

I've graduated in my faith and still I've barely pushed the gate

That opens to the one true know-it-all

My thoughts and ways are not like yours. Just as the heavens are higher than the earth, my thoughts and my ways are higher than yours.

Isaiah 55:8–9 *CEV*

What Do I Know

Marty Magehee

The mountains of Greenland loomed up through a floor of broken clouds. In only a matter of hours, my feet would walk on Russian soil—I could hardly believe it. My heart and mind felt as if they were racing in tandem. I'd never been to Europe before, much less passed through the gates of the Kremlim, and I guess you could say I was a bit over-whelmed. Centuries of history were about to become tridi-mensional. Red Square, Gorky Park, Lenin's tomb —everything from textbook entries to magazine covers would be transformed into a firsthand experience.

But somewhere beneath the thrilling rush, another sen-sation lurked. Something dark, like a bad déjà vu or a buried childhood association come back to haunt me— something that existed in me long before I left U.S. soil.

...a faith that is fervently grounded in Christ

from the album
THE RIDE

What Do I Know

I make it my firm policy
To make my bed with
    honesty
So I don't sleep with shadows in
    the room
The truth is I've been holdin' back
The way I feel about the fact
That I'm not as close as I want to
    be with You

(Channel 1)
There's still so much more of You I
    long to know
And I won't be content until I do

(Chorus)
Cause what do I know
If I don't really know You
Though I may blow the minds of
    men
How can I say that I know
Anything of love
Unless I find it in Your hands

Growing up under the influence of the American media, I'd been programmed to view the citizens of Moscow as cold, cruel, nationalistic enemies of my God and my country. So even though I'd never been there, I had a preconceived picture of who these people were and what to expect of them. All those years of NBC Nightly News and aggressive end-time evangelists had conditioned me to be suspicious of everything their country represented—that is, everything I presumed it represented.

But once we touched down and I began to meet these people face to face, my theories sprung leaks. From tour guides to hotel executives, everyone I met was warm and friendly. No one fit the molds I'd carried with me. As we passed out Bibles in the days that followed, I didn't see one cruel face, only expressions of a desperate hunger for truth and compassion. Every mental image I'd fostered over the years began to crumble. My guard melted away and I flew home a changed man.

116

I've had similar experiences in my relationship with God. It's like being in Russia all over again. Sometimes I fall into viewing myself as some kind of authority on God and his heart. If I happen to get a few spiritual victories under my belt, all of a sudden I'm sporting doctoral tassels and hanging heaven-notarized degrees on my walls. In my own mind, I am a scholar of the infinite.

Just when I'm kicked back at full recline, relishing the notion that I'm finally tuned in to the unsearchable heart of God, he lowers the lever on the recliner and sends some revealing discomfort my way. He jolts me awake with unexpected intrusions—things like sudden money problems when I supposed I was basking in divine prosperity, or marital disagreements when I was convinced I'd reached my peak as a peacemaker, or an explosion of anger when I thought I had it all together. Then, after God has allowed life to unseat me from my comfortable smugness, I regain enough presence of mind to crawl back on hands and knees to the one, true "know-it-all." And as I lift my leaking heart up for him to repair, he never says, "I told you so." Instead, he immediately opens his workshop and overwhelms me with a love I'll never understand. And I feel about him like I felt about my new Russian friends: far from knowing the depths of his heart.

On our hands and knees at the foot of God's throne is not a bad position to be in. Our spiritual survival depends on humbling ourselves before him, admitting our ignorance and weakness. We must arrive at a place where we begin to realize just how omni-everything our God is. Who wants to serve a God we can understand anyway? I know I don't. I need a heavenly Father whose love is so far

...a faith that is fervently grounded in Christ

(Vs 2)
I'm not playing playground games
I'm not reading Dick and Jane
And I don't need a pass to walk the
   halls
I've graduated in my faith
And still I've barely pushed the
   gate
That opens to the one true
   know-it-all

(Channel 2)
I could win a Nobel Prize or rule
   the world
But, I would die a genius with no
   clue

(Chorus)

(Bridge)
Life is such a cruel deception
Without You to lead my quest
I'd fail the test

(Repeat Chorus)

reaching that he is able to grant me new mercy every morning. My soul requires a God who is a never-ending source of compassion. I am finite and incapable; I need a boundless God to make me complete.

It's not for me or anyone else to figure out what is meant by "unfathomable." What is required of me is that I recognize that he is God and I am not. I rejoice in knowing that I have all of eternity to get to know him better.

Questions to Ponder

1. Has God ever lowered the lever on your recliner to remind you that you aren't the "know-it-all" you thought you were? What lessons did you learn in the process?
2. Have you ever been so humbled that you found yourself on your hands and knees before God's throne? What circumstances brought you there?
3. In view of the lessons you learned in those circumstances, was the "humiliation" worth it? Why or why not?

Back to the Basics

The basic desire in men and women to know God is a good one. We get into trouble when we think we've arrived in our relationship with him. When you spend time with God today, physically get on your knees and humbly acknowledge your lack of knowledge. Ask him to deepen your heart and expand your capacity so that you can know him better.

...a faith that is fervently grounded in Christ

Sometimes I feel like we're moving too fast
In search of the meaning of truth

I will listen to you, Lord God, because you promise
peace to those who are faithful

Psalm 85:8 *CEV*

When It Comes
to Livin'

Andy Chrisman

I have this bad habit. Every time God pulls me through
a crisis, I rejoice, testify . . . then skip my quiet time for the
next several weeks. When the crisis is passed, I don't feel
the same urgency to spend time with God that I do while
in the middle of the storm. But God spoke to me recently
and said, "Andy, if you would stay close to me when life is
running smoothly, you'd have a lot fewer problems to deal
with." So I asked him to help me find a time every day
when we could fellowship together, and then I waited to
hear from him.

Well, every morning for the next two weeks I woke up,
wide-awake, on my own, I presumed, at 5:45 A.M.—every
morning! And each time I would glance at the clock,
groan, and go back to sleep. What a fool I was. God had

...a faith that is fervently grounded in Christ

from the album
THE BASICS
OF LIFE

When It Comes to Livin'

There's only one thing that matters
    in life
In spite of the way it might seem
It's not when you're born, it's not
    when you die
But what have you done in
    between
So don't spend your days
In a useless parade of momentary
    matters
When we can change
What forever remains

(Chorus)
When it comes to livin'
We've only got one life
When it comes to dyin'
It's just a matter of time
But everybody's got a choice to
    make
For we all can make a difference in
    life

answered my prayer. He woke me up so we could spend time together, but I missed his answer fourteen straight times.

Jackie, my lovely and adoring wife, puts up with most of my male quirks—my remote-control hogging, my "I'm the man and I know best" lecturing, and my "I know exactly where I'm going" machismos. But one thing she will not tolerate is my ability to tune her out. And let me just say that if "tuning out" were a professional sport, my name would be Tiger and I'd have my own line of sports apparel.

Christians have been debating for centuries about how to recognize God when he speaks. Is it an audible voice? Is it a tonal vibration? Is it an angelic face in a tortilla in Mexico City? Jesus said in John 10:27, "My sheep know my voice; and I know them. They follow me." Only by following Jesus day in and day out, like sheep follow a shepherd, will I become familiar enough with my Shepherd's voice to recognize it in the dark. But unfortunately, I tend to listen to wrong voices now and again, and when I do tune my ear in his direction, I am too easily distracted or I listen only half-heartedly, and I miss him completely.

Not listening gets me into more trouble than just about anything else. Whenever I tune out my wife it's usually because I've given my attention over to something else— like a football game. And I do the same with God. He'll speak to me through a circumstance, through the Scriptures, or through my children, but I am so wrapped up in life's distractions that what has the potential to be a meaningful dialogue becomes a one-way conversation. I wonder how many blessings I have forfeited because I failed to really listen.

Listening to God requires my full attention, and it requires that I be quiet. I believe God is speaking his will on my life every moment, so I must pay close attention and grasp every syllable he utters. I have only one chance to live this life, and listening to what the Lord has to say is the only way for me to be sure that I'm on the right track.

What would life be like if I were so in tune to God's direction that everything I did was orchestrated by his baton? (You freewill theologians and predestinationalists may argue amongst yourselves.) The word *abundant* comes to mind (John 10:10). Such beautiful music would emanate from my life that all those around me would know that I was a man who walks with God.

I'll never forget a particular pop quiz my high school class was given one day. The teacher told us explicitly to read each of the thirty questions before we answered any of them. I skimmed through the first couple of questions, realized how easy they were and, with complete confidence, began writing down the answers. When I got down

...a faith that is fervently grounded in Christ

cont.gment>

Part Three: Faithnt>

Are you gonna take a stand for
what's right
When it comes your time

Sometimes I feel like we're moving
too fast
In search of the meaning of truth
With no place to turn and no one to
ask
I wonder just who's leading who
But time after time
There's a courage I find to stand up
to temptation
I'm building faith
With each choice that I make

(Bridge)
One thing's for certain
This crazy world is searching for a
guiding light
We can't deny that humanity is cry-
ing out
For Jesus Christ

(Chorus)

When It Comes to Livin' by Dave Clark,
Mark Harris, and Don Koch © 1992 by
John T. Benson Publishg Co./First Verse
Music/Paragon Music Corp./A-Knack-
For-This Music/Point Clear
Music/ASCAP. All rights reserved. Used
by permission.t>

to the last question, I shook my head in disgust. Number thirty was not a question at all. Instead, it read, "Do not answer questions 1–29." I didn't listen to my teacher's instructions, and I failed the test.

Listening may seem passive, inactive. But it is in our quiescence that God often displays his strength. It is in our quietness that he booms out his guidance. It is in our stillness that we hear his quiet voice. *Listen*. Listen, and you *will* hear. How many times did Jesus plead with the people of his time to open their ears and hear his words? And to those who listen, he speaks this blessing: "But God has blessed you, because your eyes can see and your ears can hear!" (Matthew 13:16).

When it comes to living . . . *listen*.

124

Questions to Ponder

1. Why is it that we feel less compelled to spend time with God when things are going good and we feel driven to him in a crisis?
2. What things distract you from listening to God?
3. When are you most in tune with God? When are you least likely to hear him?
4. What can you change about your daily routine to get quiet enough to hear God?

Back to the Basics

Determine today to set aside some quiet time just for you and God. Spend this time hearing him speak to you through his Word. Follow Christ closely so that you will know his voice when he calls you.

...a faith that is fervently grounded in Christ

There's no containing this great move of restoration

It knows no walls, no boundaries or lines

> Later I will give my Spirit to everyone. Your sons and
> daughters will prophesy. Your old men will have
> dreams and your young men will see visions.

Joel 2:28 CEV

....

Great Awakening

Kirk Sullivan

Sunday morning, Sunday night, Tuesday night, and Thursday night—week in and week out, month after month, our family was at church. It was a rare occasion that we ever missed a service. I was raised in a small Pentecostal church, and looking back on my upbringing, I'm thankful and proud of my Pentecostal heritage. My dad told me that when he was a little boy, he thought his church was called Pentecostal because it cost a penny to get in. You see, his mother would always give him a penny to put in the offering, and he thought the penny was payment—get it, "penny-cost."

I was often teased as a teenager for my "religious heritage." When my buddies and I talked about where we went to church, I tried to explain my church without saying

...a faith that is fervently grounded in Christ

from the album
O B V I O U S

Great Awakening

Here in this moment in time
We search for wonders for
    miracles and signs
Something to satisfy the hunger in
    us all
A human rage from deep within the
    soul

Like a machine in pursuit
On the horizon like a raging fire we
    move
Driven by questions in an endless
    search for truth
There is a stirring in us
A great awakening begins

(Chorus)
I believe there's a mighty power
I believe it's a latter rain
I believe there's a move of God
Calling us all higher, oh I believe
These are the days of the great
    awakening

"Pentecostal" outright. But it would always come out somehow, and one of the guys would end up saying, "Ooooh, you go to that church where they swing from the chandeliers and jump over pews!" But it was all in good fun, and I survived.

But the world has gotten a lot more complicated since I was a teen. Multitudes of people are devastated by sin and its impact in the world. Lives are torn apart; people are depressed and without hope. Many struggle with addictions of all sorts. Even God's elect suffer the effects of sin. What church has escaped the pain and confusion of divorce? What church has not seen the breakdown of morality among its own people?

Even so, God is pouring himself out on mankind. In this hour, when people are consumed with trying to fill the void in their lives, God's Spirit is moving in a mighty way. My pastor recently said that more people have accepted Christ in the last five years than in the entire history of

Christendom. There is a great awakening going on, and I want to be a part of it.

Living only forty-five minutes from Pensacola, Florida, and the "Brownsville Revival," I have attended several revival services. I realize there is some discussion about some of the things that are occurring at Brownsville, but this much is certain: lives are being changed for God. On occasion, people who have heard the message of Jesus but have never given their hearts to him make decisions for Christ in the lobby with the help of Christian counselors before they ever make it into the sanctuary. God is moving not only in Brownsville, but all over the world.

God is moving in inner-city ministries, enabling spiritually bereft people to turn their lives around. Children who daily witnessed violence and abuse are now seeing their parents changed by the power of God. People are getting off welfare and becoming models for their communities. A great awakening is taking place in urban areas.

God is also doing an amazing work on college campuses. Young people are taking their commitment to God seriously, as they struggle with the concept of what Jesus would do if he were in their place. And they are finding ways to give their lives away for Christ.

Even in the music world we see a great awakening. Christian music is impacting more than ever before. Large venues are packed with audiences wanting to hear music that affirms Jesus.

The working of God is certainly not confined to the United States. Thousands of people in Russia and other formerly communist countries are searching for God. Mul-

...a faith that is fervently grounded in Christ

More than our hearts can contain
It is an overflow of God's amazing
  grace
Coming to reconcile a world that's
  lost it way
Oh, all consuming fire
Come purify us once again

(Chorus)

(Bridge)
There's no containing this great
  move of restoration
It knows no walls, no boundaries or
  lines
Without a doubt I do believe if we'll
  just get down on our knees
The latter rain is gonna fall, it's just
a matter of time

(Chorus)

titudes are responding to the message of Jesus throughout South America and Africa.

People all over the world are being awakened from spiritual complacency. God is calling us to walk closer to him and to know him more intimately. He is calling us to remove the things in our lives that hinder our relationship with him. He is coming into our lives to heal our secret pain and to release us from fear so that we can walk in true freedom. I want that freedom in my life. I want to be a part of what God is doing among us. But I understand that I can have these blessings only if I get on my knees and seek God's face.

Revival always begins with God's people on their knees, and that is where you and I must be if we want to be a part of the work of God in these times. We must begin by humbling ourselves before God, by confessing our unworthiness and our complete dependence on him.

There is an unrest in the world like never before, and I believe that unrest is a result of God's stirring among us. He is calling us to a higher place. He wants to consume us, to purify us, to make us the spotless bride of Christ. Let's pray for God's outpouring in our homes and churches. Let's be in the center of what God is doing, instead of hanging fearfully to the outside edges. Let's open ourselves up to receive everything he has promised. I don't know all that God has planned for me, but I do know that I don't want to be sleeping as he pours out his blessings; I want to be a part of the Great Awakening.

Questions to Ponder

1. What evidence do you see of God moving in this present time?
2. What does it mean to seek God's face? Read the following Scriptures for a better understanding: 1 Chronicles 16:11; 2 Chronicles 7:14; Psalm 27:8; Psalm 105:4.
3. Has spiritual complacency crept into your life? What can you do to open your heart to the Lord's awakening?

Back to the Basics

From the beginning of time, God has moved among the lives of his people—that's one of the basics of the Christian walk. If we are to be a part of his movement now, we must begin by letting him direct us. Instead of asking for something from God, ask him what he would have you know and do. Ask him to show you his will for your life.

...a faith that is fervently grounded in Christ

God looks through the surface

And He defines your worth by what is on the inside

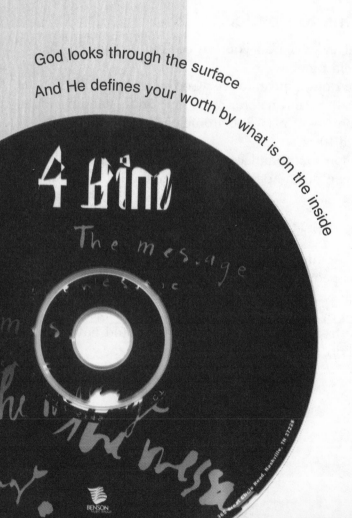

4 Him

The message

BENSON
Music Group

365 Great Circle Road, Nashville, TN 37228

I want you to know all about Christ's love, although it
is too wonderful to be measured. Then your
lives will be filled with all that God is.

Ephesians 3:19 *CEV*

The Measure
of a Man

Mark Harris

Where was Bubba? For thirty years he had welcomed
them as they turned into the parking lot in downtown
Mobile. Working as the maintenance man at McGowan
Lines hardware store, Bubba was always the first one to
arrive at 5:30 A.M. And every morning he was out in the
parking lot as the bankers, lawyers, doctors, politicians,
and businessmen arrived for work in nearby business
buildings. Every morning he greeted them with a smile
and a nod. They could always depend on Bubba being
there to welcome them to a new day.

But on this Thursday morning in 1959, Bubba wasn't
there. Bubba had passed away the night before. Bubba had
gotten his wish. He'd always said that when it came his
time to go, he hoped he'd go in his sleep.

...a faith that is fervently grounded in Christ

from the album
THE MESSAGE

The Measure of a Man

This world can analyze and size
    you up
And throw you on the scales
They can IQ you and run you
    through
Their rigorous details
They can do their best to rate you
And they'll place you on their
    charts
And then back it up with scientific
    smarts
But there's more to what you're
    worth
Than what human eyes can see

(Chorus)
Oh I say the measure of a man
Is not how tall you stand
How wealthy or intelligent you are
'Cause I found out the measure of
    a man
God knows and understands
For He looks inside to the bottom
    of your heart

I never got to meet Bubba. He died three years before I was born. But I heard a lot about him. People who knew him say he whistled and sang and had a smile on his face every minute of the day. Bubba wasn't a success by worldly standards. He was a lower-class, blue-collar, working man with seven kids, living in a government housing project in southern Alabama. If I had to combine all the descriptions of Bubba into one sentence, it would be, "Bubba loved telling people about Jesus, because Bubba loved Jesus." A simple description of a simple man. Yet no greater epitaph could a man have.

Bubba left no great fortune when he died, but to those who knew him, he left a legacy that lives to this very day—a legacy of which I am a part. Thousands of people called him Bubba; I call him Grandpa Harris.

I've wondered a thousand times what it would have been like to know him. Everyone who knew him says he was an incredible man. He had a magnetic quality that drew people to him; everyone who knew him wanted to be around him. There is no telling how many people all over the Southeast came to know Christ because of Bubba's witness.

It amazes me that a man who had to tape cardboard to the bottom of his shoes to cover the holes in them would be able to whistle through his daily routine. Many people spend their lives building financial empires. Bubba invested his life in *people*, building the kingdom of God.

According to worldly standards, my grandpa didn't measure up to much of a man. He amassed no great fortune, held no prominent position, and earned no Ph.D. But an overflow crowd came to honor him at his funeral. They came not to honor a man of material wealth; they came to honor a man whose heart reflected Christ's. Out of the overflow of his heart, he had shared the love of God with all he met; and on that day, they honored what he shared.

Bubba's life is a shining example for me. The simple, straightforward focus of his life reminds me of what's truly important. When I search my life and imagine myself being measured in God's grand scale, my thoughts go to Grandpa Harris, and humbled, I set about reprioritizing my life . . . again. Whether we want to admit it or not, the priorities of our lives define who we are. If we want to be remembered as Christ-honoring men and women, we must be so full of Christ that others can see him living in us. My grandpa will forever be remembered as "that Christian maintenance man at McGowan Lines who loved to smile, whistle, and sing." My prayer is that when people measure my life they will say, "He was a Christian man who sang and wrote songs to honor his Lord."

..a faith that is fervently grounded in Christ

And what's in the heart defines
The measure of a man

Well you can doubt your worth
And search for who you are and
  where you stand
But God made you in His image
When He formed you in His hands
And He looks at you with mercy
And He sees you through His love
You're His child and that will always
  be enough
For there's more to what you're
  worth
Than you could ever comprehend

(Chorus)

(Bridge)
You can spend your life pursuing
  physical perfection
There is so much more, more than
  ever meets the eye
For God looks through the surface
And He defines your worth by
  what is on the inside

(Chorus)

The Measure of a Man by Mark Harris, Don
Koch, and Stephanie Lewis © 1996 Paragon
MusicCorp./Point Clear Music/ASCAP/Defini-
tive Music (admin. by Word, Inc.)/Dayspring
Music (a div. of Word, Inc.)/BMI/Birdwing
Music (admin. by EMI Christian Music Publish-
ing)/ASCAP. All rights reserved. Used by per-
mission.

Questions to Ponder

1. How do you want people to remember you after you are gone?
2. Are you living your life now in a way that will leave the legacy you desire?
3. Make a list of the five most important things/people in your life. Cross off three. What remains? Are these priorities the ones you want to be remembered by?

Back to the Basics

Look at the two items that remain on your list from question number three, above. Are these two items things you would call "basics of life"? Whatever is on your list, commit your list to God and ask him to help you align your priorities with his.

..a faith that is fervently grounded in Christ

Where there is faith there is a voice calling, keep walking

Where there is faith there is a peace like a child sleeping

4HIM

S10X-007013

BENSON

COMPACT
DIGITAL AUDIO

id

or You

aith

Bread Of Life *

n **

Am Gone

Produced by Don Koch
Produced by Jonathan David Brown *
Produced by Chris Harris and
Mark Heimermann for
Funattic Productions **

*The Lord is your protector, and he won't go
to sleep or let you stumble.*

Psalm 121:3 CEV

Where There Is Faith

Andy Chrisman

I love watching my children sleep. Jackie can always count on me to volunteer for final bed check at night. I bound up the stairs and turn into Lucas's room first. His head is always securely on his pillow and the covers are tucked neatly under his chin. I turn off his closet light and his CD player and make my way toward Kayleigh's room, praying I don't step on Mr. Potato Head in the dark. As she sleeps soundly in her baby bed, she looks as if she's just passed out in mid-motion. Her arms and legs are pointing in all directions, and there's no blanket or pillow in sight. No lights or music to turn off in here. Unlike her brother, those things only keep her awake. My children's methods of getting to sleep mirror their personalities—one needs a diversion, the other wants to be left alone. But they both

139

..a faith that is fervently grounded in Christ

Part Three: Faith

from the album
4 H I M

Where
There Is
Faith

I believe in faithfulness
I believe in giving of myself for
     someone else
I believe in peace and love
I believe in honesty and trust but it's
     not enough
For all that I believe may never
     change the way it is
Unless I believe Jesus lives

(Chorus)
Where there is faith
There is a voice calling, keep
     walking
You're not alone in this world
Where there is faith
There is a peace like a child sleeping
Hope everlasting in He who is able
     to
Bear every burden, to heal every
     hurt in my heart

sleep so peacefully. And that's what compels me each night to make that last dash up the stairs to gaze at their sweet, sleeping faces.

I'm learning that peace flourishes only in the absence of fear. Lucas and Kayleigh haven't yet learned how to be afraid of disaster. They live day to day, dwelling on the enjoyment of each adventure they create. They're not worried about tomorrow, whether they'll have enough food or if the stock market will hold its value (Matthew 6:31, 34). My little darlings are also not afraid of waking their parents at 3 A.M. if they need something. I doubt they think, "Hmmm . . . I've asked a lot of Mom today. She's probably tired of hearing my voice." Not a chance! Hesitation is nonexistent in my children. They need; they ask; they receive (Matthew 7:7–8).

How many times has the fear of rejection robbed you of the solace your heart so desperately need? You've asked him for so

140

much lately that you hate to disturb him again. What if he's tired of hearing your desperate pleas? Do you wonder if he thinks, "Oh no, not again! Can't I go just one day without my child bothering me"? Not a chance! The key is that you are God's *child*. What decent parent refuses to meet the needs of his or her most prized possession? And God is more than a decent father—he's the best ever. He definitely knows how to kiss a boo-boo and make it better, he always has time for you, and he doesn't ever sleep (Psalm 121:3–4). He disciplines only out of love, never out of anger (Revelation 3:19), and you couldn't begin to count the number of times he's thought about you today (Psalm 139:17–18). You—and all your brothers and sisters—are the most important thing to him. He even gave away his most precious possession just so he could have you sleeping upstairs in his house forever.

Replace your fear of failure with the peace of knowing that Daddy owns the store and you can have anything you need, anytime you need it. Don't be afraid to ask. He'll be thrilled to hear from you. So close your eyes and get some rest—he's got a big day planned for you tomorrow. And if you should need him during the night, he'll be there before you can say, "Daddy, can I have a drink of water . . ."

..a faith that is fervently grounded in Christ

It is a wonderful, powerful place
Where there is faith

There's a man across the sea
Never heard the sound of freedom
    ring
Only in his dreams
There's a lady dressed in black
In a motorcade of cadillacs
Daddy's not coming back
Our hearts begin to fall
And our stability grows weak
But Jesus meets our needs if only
    we believe

(Chorus)

Questions to Ponder

1. What fears keep you from knowing the peace of God?
2. What is it about God's love that most encourages you to approach him in prayer?
3. Since God is our Father, what special privileges do we have as his children?
4. What hurts would you like to take to your gentle, heavenly Father?

Back to the Basics

Jesus said that "you cannot get into God's kingdom unless you accept it the way a child does" (Mark 10:15). Think about how a child receives something given to him or her. Try to imagine yourself as a child in the presence of God as he gives you the gifts of abundant life. Put aside your fears and receive what he offers with peace and assurance, knowing that his love is unconditional and everlasting.

..a faith that is fervently grounded in Christ

How many times have you called for me
When my heart was willing but I was so weak

Abraham had faith and obeyed God. He was told to go to the
land God had said would be his. . . . Abraham did this,
because he was waiting for the eternal city
that God had planned and built.

Hebrews 11:8, 10 *CEV*

As Long as My Heart
Knows It's You

Kirk Sullivan

I graduated from high school on May 24, 1977. It doesn't
seem possible that I've been out of school for over twenty
years! In August of that same year, God called me to go on
the road, something he had been preparing me to do for the
last eighteen years.

Over the last several years, many people have asked me
how my life in ministry started. If you're standing, please
be seated.

I grew up in a small Assembly of God church in South
Oklahoma City. My mother was the church pianist even
before my parents met. My grandpa was the head deacon
for thirty years, and my grandma played guitar in the
church orchestra. In other words, I grew up on the front
pew. As soon as I started talking, I was singing. I sang in

..*a faith that is fervently grounded in Christ*

from the album
THE RIDE

As Long as My Heart Knows It's You

God only knows how he must have
    felt
Out on the mountain where
    Abraham knelt
Though deep in his heart I'm sure it
    hurt to obey
Still he offered his son as if to
    say, I'm

Willing to live
Willing to die
Willing to make any sacrifice
I'm willing to go
Willing to stay
Lord, there's no price too high for
    me to pay
Any struggle that might come my
    way
I'm willing to go through

church weddings, funerals, and all my mother's piano recitals.

It wasn't long before my parents realized that I had a calling on my life. I remember hearing the call as a small boy. No, I didn't hear an audible voice, but I did feel a burning desire to sing, to express with my voice what I felt in my heart. Whenever a group or soloist came to our church to sing, it took all the restraint I could muster to keep from jumping up on the stage with them; and as I got older, the desire became stronger.

A few months after I graduated from high school, I came in contact with a group that traveled full time. They needed a singer, so I auditioned and got the part. I came home with the exciting news, expecting my parents to be elated. To say the least, they were not! Of course they wanted the best for me, and to them that meant college—not a career of singing on the road. Home life was quite difficult for the next several days. Although my mother never told me I couldn't go, she did give me lots of reasons why I should go to college instead.

I'll never forget the morning I was supposed to register for college. When Mom came into my room, I was expecting a barrage of reasons I should go register. Instead, she told me of her experience the night before. She had waked up in the middle of the night, still in turmoil over the discussions of the last few days. She felt impressed to read her Bible, and when she opened it, it opened to Psalm 150, which speaks of praising the Lord with horns, stringed instruments, and cymbals. It was then that she felt the Lord speaking to her, telling her that this was the appointed time for me to begin fulfilling the calling on my life.

As I look to Scripture, I see many people who had to make tough decisions that affected their lives dramatically. Can you imagine the agony Abraham experienced when God asked him to offer his son Isaac as an offering? I'm sure Isaac meant more to his father than anything, but Abraham was obedient when God called him. And how must Mary have felt as she watched Jesus being led to the Cross, fulfilling the ministry for which he had come to earth.

God has a purpose for you too. While he hasn't called any of us to sacrifice ourselves or our children on an altar or a cross, he does have a plan for each of our lives. And he prepares us for whatever that purpose is. Fulfilling his purpose fills us with peace, not with fear. If you think God is calling you to do or be something, but your heart if filled with fear, I tell you from experience that that calling is not from God.

..a faith that is fervently grounded in Christ

Just as long as my heart
As long as my heart knows it's you.

How many times have you called
    for me
When my heart was willing but I
    was so weak
What I would give if I could only
    believe
That when I'm tested by fire I'll
    always be

"Willing to live, willing to die, willing to make any sacrifice"—these words from "As Long as My Heart Knows It's You" are not easy to live out. But if we have faith to do what God has called us to do, he will be faithful to empower us and give us peace, and he will give us the faith we need to answer his call. Then we can say, "I'll do what you want me to do, I'll go where you want me to go, as long as my heart knows it's you."

Questions to Ponder

1. Have you ever felt called of God for a specific work? How did you respond?
2. What decisions have made that affected your life for many years? Do you think you made the decision God wanted you to make?
3. Is there something you feel called of God to do that is difficult? How can knowing that it is God who is calling help you follow through?

Back to the Basics

Making basic decisions that affect the whole direction of your life can be quite frightening. Sometimes we're tempted to tell God what we want to happen and ask him to work it out. The next time you have a major life-decision to make, instead of asking God for a specific out-come, ask that his "perfect will be done in your life." This takes all the faith you can muster, but when you submit wholly to his will, he will use you marvelously for his glory.

...a faith that is fervently grounded in Christ

A constant struggle just to sit on the side

My own ambition tells me I gotta drive

With all your heart you must trust the Lord and not
your own judgement. Always let him lead you, and
he will clear the road for you to follow.

Proverbs 3:5–6 *CEV*

....

Who's at the Wheel

Marty Magehee

It was May of '86, and the past four years of my life
were fading in my rear view mirror as I drove away from
my alma mater, Evangel College. All it had taken to turn
that significant portion of my life into a memory was a
short walk and a simple handshake.

Laying in the passenger seat, still rolled and bound by
a blue ribbon, was the piece of paper I had worked so hard
to win. I was convinced it was my ticket to the future. I
picked it up and held it in my hand; I finally had a firm
grasp on my future. I felt as if the whole world were in the
palm of my hand. There was no doubt in my mind that I
was on my way to bigger and better—my life was truly
beginning to make sense.

...a faith that is fervently grounded in Christ

from the album
O B V I O U S

Who's at
the Wheel

Out on this narrow road
Eyeing every exit sign
I wanna take control
Running this race through my mind

(Channel)
A constant struggle just to sit on
the side
My own ambition tells me I gotta
drive
But the key that turns my soul
Tells me who's king of this road

(Chorus)
Who keeps your life between the
lines
Tell me who's at the wheel
When left is wrong who steers it
right
Tell me who's at the wheel

Here in this great unknown
Traveling day and night
These wheels are not our own
We're just along for the ride

Six months later, I sat staring
at the walls of my basement bed-
room, without a clue as to what I
wanted to do with the rest of my
life. I was living in the bottom of
my ex-roommate's parents'
house. I'd tried everything from
selling alarm systems to working
with ten elderly women as a
phone rep for the Missouri
Department of Tourism. Nothing
seemed to click. Dead ends
blocked my progress at every
turn. It was as if the map I had
drawn for my life had suddenly
been erased, and I didn't have
the slightest inkling why.

My ace-in-the-hole had been
my B.A. in music education, but
somewhere along the way, I had
lost my drive to teach. At one
point I thought I'd like to work as
a music minister in a church, but
that role no longer appealed to
me. I loved to write and sing, but
I didn't have the first clue as to
how to make a career of it. So,
there I sat, suspended in my own
no man's land, facing a life without direction.

What had gone wrong? Only a
few months earlier, I had been

exploding with ideas. While I was on campus at Evangel, there hadn't been a moment when I didn't feel I had everything under control—my grades, my classes, my health, my social life. Why should my future be any different? But here I was at a total impasse, without even a hint of a career. Numb and defeated, I packed my things and headed back home.

I'll never forget that perplexing drive home eleven years ago. The impression it made on my life changed me forever. God knew how hardheaded and driven I was; he knew that the only way to convince me of the blessedness of surrender was to let me learn it the hard way.

Now, after being on the road for more than a decade, I've heard story after story of recent graduates who struggled through a scenario similar to mine. It's amazing how often we as Christians, while claiming Jesus as Lord, still try to map out our own lives without leaving any room for divine guidance. Human ambition can be a dangerous thing. We set ourselves up for a fall when we rely on our diplomas, money, or achievements to secure our future. The sense of security they give us proves false every time.

There's a really good reason that the future is called the "great unknown." Matthew 6:27 tells us that we can't even add one hour to our life span, much less control our destiny. The minute we plop ourselves in the driver's seat and push the pedal to the floor, we being moving backwards—and yet we continue to put ourselves at the wheel. I still do it, more times than I care to mention.

Much of our impulse to be in control stems from living in a country that promotes self-actualization. We're programmed to believe that if we're not worrying about the problem or taking control of the situation, we're incompetent,

...a faith that is fervently grounded in Christ

(Channel)
Life is a journey of the choices we
    make
I'll rediscover every mile of the way
That there's only one way home
It's riding with the king of the this
    road

(Chorus)

(Bridge)
The wheels are turning faster than
    they ever have before
The lights are flashing warning
    signs that we just
Can't ignore
We've the pedal to the floor

(Chorus)

weak, and irresponsible. What a
joke. God's message could not be
more opposite from the world's.
The only proactive role we are to
play in the struggles and dreams
of our day-to-day experience is to
hand the seat of command over
to the one who holds the keys to
us all.

It wasn't until I went back
home after college that I really
began to listen to God's leading.
He spoke to me through the wisdom of a Christian mom and
dad, as he gently inched me over
to the passenger seat and showed
me the thrills of a trip navigated
by his will.

I'm still hardheaded, and I still
find myself grabbing for the
wheel every now and then, but
with every mile, I'm learning
more abut the sweet release that
comes only from letting God be
God.

Questions to Ponder

1. Can you think of an experience in your life where you were forced to let God take control of the wheel? How did things change after you gave him control?
2. What things/accomplishments have you relied on to bring security and order to your life? Did they bring you the security you wanted? What happened?
3. Who has God used in your life to inch you into the passenger seat?
4. Is there something in your life right now that you need to hand over to him?

Back to the Basics

Control is definitely one of the basic issues of life. We all want it, and we usually feel insecure when someone else has it. When we lose control, we begin to learn that it all boils down to trust. While no one on this earth is completely trustworthy, our heavenly Father is. Take whatever it is that you are trying to "manage" on your own, lay it at his feet, and ask him to give you the strength not to pick it back up again. He can create trust in your fearful heart—just ask him.

..a faith that is fervently grounded in Christ...

PART FOUR

...the

hope

that endures for all times

But I, I'm longing for the day

When my mysteries of You will be erased

> I will explain a mystery to you. Not every one
> of us will die, but we will all be changed.
>
> 1 Corinthians 15:51 *CEV*

Mystery of Grace

Andy Chrisman

Grace passed away last week. She was ninety-two. She was also my last grandparent. I got the phone call from my mom, who was at Granny's bedside. The funeral was short and sweet, and as we moved from the funeral home to the cemetery, the reality that Granny Grace was gone began to set in. The pastor wrapped up the service by praying and blessing the family, and my father and I spontaneously broke into the same song my brother Jerry and I sang to Granny at her ninetieth birthday party. By the end of the chorus, everyone there was honoring my mother's mother with the song that bore her name—"Amazing Grace."

I have yet to cry for Granny. She lived a lot longer than most. She was active and mobile until a week before she passed on; and best of all, she was ready. She had no fear

...the hope that endures for all times

159

from the album
O B V I O U S

Mystery of Grace

A solitary picture hanging on my
   wall
The same familiar scenery we all
   have seen before
And I can't help but wonder
Staring at Your face
Just what You must have been like
As You visited this place
God come to earth as man to save
   us all

But I, I'm longing for the day
When my mysteries of You will be
   erased
But until then
I must go on living (until then)
This world will keep on spinning
   (until then)
Until then I'll live by faith

(Chorus)
Oh the mystery of grace
Will someday be erased
When I see You face to face
In heaven some sweet day

of leaving this world and going on to the next realm. She no longer wonders what Jesus looks like. She now knows how the universe was created. She's been enlightened as to why things happened the way they did during her life. Her body is perfect now—no aches, pains, or wrinkles. She knows more now than all the scientists, doctors, and theologians on this planet combined. No more mysteries for Grace Brown—or whatever God calls her now. No way she's coming back here. Why would she want to?

Granny's death provided a great opportunity to explain to Lucas, my five-year-old, about what happens when we die. He was standing in the room when we got the phone call about G.G., and he immediately sensed the sadness in my wife's and my expressions.

"So, I can't call her on the phone anymore?" he asked.

"No, I'm sorry, Lucas, but Granny Grace doesn't live in Missouri anymore. She's gone to live way up in heaven with Jesus. She left about ten minutes ago."

Lucas pondered that thought for a moment, looking off into the distance. "Oh, she went to Canada," he deduced. "That's very high above Missouri." My son, the geography whiz.

"Will I ever see her again, Daddy?"

"Of course you will. You'll be in heaven with her one day," I told him.

"But, I'll be a thousand years old by then," my little carbon copy said, with a measure of sadness in his voice.

Oh Lord, how I pray my children would live that long—or at least long enough to do everything they've been created to do (and maybe an extra fifty years for good measure).

A part of me longs to know what G.G. knows right now, to lay prostrate in the presence of God, to really understand how our Creator could love us so much, to live in perfection. But I'm not ready to go yet. There's too much love left in me to give to my wife and my children, so much more grace to experience.

> Until then, I'll live by faith.
> Oh, the mystery of grace
> Will someday be erased,
> When I see You face to face,
> In heaven some sweet day.

For Grace, the mystery is gone.

...the hope that endures for all times

Now I've got all Your letters
I read them everyday
I'm finding more and more
I hang on every word You say
I've often called You friend
And I can't forget

That You, You are making me a
   place
Far beyond this present madness
   that I face
But until then
I must go on living (until then)
I'll keep hanging on from day to day
   (until then)
Until then I'll live by faith

(Chorus)

Questions to Ponder

1. What mysteries do you look forward to understanding someday?
2. What loved one of yours has already gone on to be with God? What mysteries do you think are now clear for that person?
3. How does imagining what God has in store for you change your view of death?

Back to the Basics

Death is such a basic part of life, yet it often takes us by surprise when it comes to someone we love. Even though death is an instrument of Satan, God has the final victory through the resurrection. Read 1 Corinthians 15 to gain a better, basic understanding of death and the resurrection promise.

...the hope that endures for all times

Hold tight for we are promised in time

Those who patiently wait will never wait in vain

The Lord's people may suffer a lot, but he
will always bring them safely through.

Psalm 34:19 *CEV*

Shelter in the Rain

Marty Magehee

I was in agony, hobbling through paradise. Only two days had passed since Sheri and I arrived in St. Lucia, West Indies, for our first-year wedding anniversary/honeymoon. And now, I was consumed with an overwhelming, acute pain from my knees to my toes. Intense, sharp, stabbing sensations permeated the core of every joint. I was as confused as I was miserable.

It had all begun earlier that morning, September 20, 1994, somewhere around 3:00 A.M., when I woke up shaking violently. There, surrounded by the moist warmth of the lush tropic, my teeth were chattering like a child pulled from an ice break in a frozen lake. A mysterious chilling wave had suddenly washed through my entire frame, nailing me to my bed sheets. And then another sensation—

...the hope that endures for all times

from the album
THE RIDE

Shelter in the Rain

How long have you been waiting on
  a little sun to shine
To take away the night
Hold on, for you are never alone
  through the darkest skies
There is a guiding light
For our God is a refuge
Where the weary can run and hide
  in times of trouble
He'll be the calm in the midst of the
  storm
Till it passes by
Oh, you need to know

(Chorus)
There's a shelter in the rain
There's a hope for your tomorrow
There's a cover through the pain
When you're underneath the
  weather
Jesus is the shelter in the rain

Sometimes when hope is hard to
  find we've got to walk by faith
Until we see the way

much like an army of tiny spiders racing through my veins—began to rush the full length of my legs. Both symptoms seemed to swirl in and out of each other, creating an eerie state of awareness that pinned me between nightmare and reality in a sort of swooning delirium. Sheri wrapped herself around me in a desperate attempt to restore warmth and calm to my shivering body. After she held me for several minutes, we both turned onto our backs and stared trance-like up at the ceiling, shaken to our cores by this unexpected unknown. Only one thing was for certain: something much darker than the thick Caribbean night had broken into our lives.

As the week progressed, my ankles become less human-like, swelling to twice their original size. I weighed every painful step one at a time, praying that the following step wouldn't hurt as badly as the one before. Without Sheri's shoulder, I would have been as languid as a slug. Whenever I'd catch our slow-motion shadows on a walkway or wall, a debilitating sense of helplessness would fall over me. At times, I felt as if the spirit of Norman Rockwell was hovering nearby, perched behind his easel, painting our silhouettes as a geriatrics nurse and her feeble patient. The pace of our young lives had slowed drastically, painfully, without any warning.

Four days and eleven doctors after returning to the States, I was finally diagnosed with a rare form of arthritis that originated from a genetic disorder I'd inherited from my mother's side of the family. The doctors said there was a whopping 25 percent chance that I would ever experience a relatively painless day; and, in the unlikely event that I ended up falling within that fortunate percentile, they seriously doubted that I would ever regain the ability to walk normally. I was faced with the prospect of rediscovering familiar territory from the vantage point of a wheelchair. I couldn't believe this was happening. One year and two passionate vows earlier, Sheri and I would have never—in our wildest, most twisted imaginations—expected that she would be wheeling me through life so soon. It was a bit much for us to comprehend.

Through a lot of prayer, effort, and Sheri's true love, I worked my way to crutches in less that two months. As the medicine began to get into my system and take effect, I eventually left the crutches for an occasional cane, handrail, ledge, or whatever else I could find to serve the moment. But even with that bit of progress, the pain lingered and my weight continued to drop. It was a struggle just to get out of bed in the mornings, and then after I managed to get up, I faced the prospect of muddling through another defeating day. It was an ever-present reality—not just a bad dream. But the peace of God became my cloud

...the hope that endures for all times

Hold tight for we are promised in
    time those who patiently wait
Will never wait in vain
For we know God is faithful
He's a fortress to run into
In times of trouble
He'll cover us with the wings of His
    love
Till we make it through
Oh, we got to know

(Chorus)

(Bridge)
So tell me why, why could you ever
    run away
From the cover out into the storm
Just know in time the rain's gonna
    bring a brighter day
And the clouds will be gone but
    while you wait on the Lord

by day and my fire by night. If
not for his constant presence, I
probably would have wound up
nestled in the dimly lit corner of a
padded room somewhere.

Prayers went up to the Father
continually. Sheri and I were in
prayer several times a day, and
friends across the country let us
know they were faithfully taking
me before the throne. Then at
around 6:45 P.M., Eastern Stan-
dard Time on March 14, 1995—
seven months after that horrible
night in the Caribbean, 4HIM was
moments away from giving a
concert at Black Hawk Baptist
Church in Ft. Wayne, Indiana. As
I was making my way from the
dressing room to the stage, I
descended the first of two flights
of stairs—the same stairs I'd
labored to climb earlier that day. I
stopped abruptly on the middle
landing. Something had happened. The pain . . . where was
the pain? I took the second flight
expecting the delusion to end
and reality to kick in, but it never
did. I literally glided down each
step, feeling light, almost buoy-
ant—and no pain!

Throughout the concert, I felt as if I were floating on air. I bounced, nearly flying, from one end of the stage to the other, like a prisoner of war cut free from his manacles, dancing on his native soil. I was completely healed. Set free. Delivered. Instantaneously, my heavenly Father lifted every dark shroud, every weight, every smoke-and-mirrored lie of the enemy, and restored a renewed sense of hope and health to my life. Hallelujah! Our God is faithful and true.

To say that my life has changed because of this experience is a given. To say that I've learned the blessings of embracing the storms in my life is a little harder to grasp. We humans don't have the inherent ability to readily accept the physical pains and hardships that our enemy constantly hurls in our paths. This is why Jesus encourages us to persevere with these words: "I give you peace, the kind of peace that only I can give. It isn't like the peace that this world can give. So don't be worried or afraid" (John 14:27).

Jesus knew that every one of us needs a powerful promise of peace to transcend the effects of life's inevitable trials. Satan casts a dark shadow over our fallen world, and the pain he inflicts on us can shake our faith and send us running for the hills. But God is our shelter when Satan sends the winds and rains. He is still in control as our ultimate protector. True to his nature as a loving and redeeming God, he can take any horror of Satan and bring good from it.

For me, he became a covering through the pain—not from the pain. He gave me the strength I needed to endure what he permitted the prince of this world to blow into my life, and then he centered me in the grip of his will

...the hope that endures for all times

with a peace that shattered every shred of my logic. Second Corinthians 4:16–17 says it best:

> We never give up. Our bodies are gradually dying, but we ourselves are being made stronger each day. These little troubles are getting us ready for an eternal glory that will make all our troubles seem like nothing.

In sharing all of this, I am in no way implying that everyone has to walk the wilderness I walked. God's design for each of us is as varied as the patterns on the tips of our fingers. As a matter of fact, there are many reading this who may never have to explore the limits of pain's dark threshold; while others who might be living under the same roof have to journey its jagged edges every day. Who are we to question God's sovereignty? His motives are purely love, and his ultimate plans are always to give us hope and a future. It's never a cruel and sadistic game with him. If we agree to forget our petty pride, humble ourselves to his blueprint, and wait on him in even the strongest of gales, he's promised to restore everything we might lose along the way and lift us up at the appropriate time. Psalm 34:19 says, "The Lord's people may suffer a lot, but he will always bring them safely through." Whether it means remaining here or going to be with him, his rainbow of deliverance is always a sure thing.

If I had to relive my St. Lucian nightmare, with the choice to alter any part of it, I don't think I would shield one drop of rain. In looking back I've realized that I'd found my pot of gold long before the rainbow was even drawn. Not only has my experience become a treasured testimony that encourages everyone who hears it, but it's given my roots the chance to go deeper than I'd ever dreamed. If it wasn't for the storms, I wouldn't have the vision to see just how brightly these days of his blessed grace are now shining in my life.

Questions to Ponder

1. Have you or anyone close to you ever experienced a physically debilitating illness? What, if anything, about my experience do you relate to?
2. Have you ever had an experience where God's strength was the only strength you had?
3. Does it make sense to you that God can walk with us though our pain without removing the pain? Can you look back at a painful time in your life and see God's footprints beside you in your pain?
4. What evidence do you see in your life that God can take any of Satan's horrors and bring good from them?

Back to the Basics

The sources of pain are many. Sometimes our pain is the result of our own sin, sometimes it is the result of someone else's. But more often, we are afflicted with pain simply because we live in a fallen world. One of the basic issues of pain that must be dealt with is blame. When we hurt, we want to blame someone—ourselves, someone else, God. One of the basic lessons of life is that no matter the source of pain, Satan is to blame. But if we cling to the hope born of heaven and if we trust in the promise of God's peace, whether in this life or the one to come, deliverance is inevitable.

...the hope that endures for all times

The Lord has never been afraid of honest prayers
And He won't allow the burden to be more than you can bear

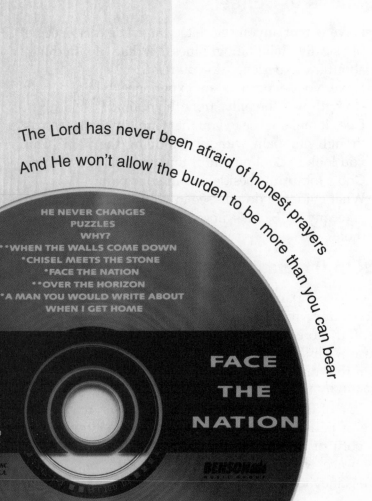

HE NEVER CHANGES
PUZZLES
WHY?
**WHEN THE WALLS COME DOWN
*CHISEL MEETS THE STONE
*FACE THE NATION
**OVER THE HORIZON
**A MAN YOU WOULD WRITE ABOUT
WHEN I GET HOME

FACE
THE
NATION

MUSIC GROUP INC.
ade in the U.S.A.

BENSON
MUSIC GROUP

EVERY REASON TO BELIEVE
*TAKE ME TO THE PLACE
WHEN I GET HOME (REPRISE)

Produced by: Don Koch
*Produced by: Chris Harris for Funattic Productions
**Produced by: Reed Arvin for Casa de Pepe Music
Executive Producer: Andy Ivey

Why?

Mark Harris

It all began on a bright, sunny, Tennessee day on the campus of Lee College where Matt and I were students. We had been best of friends for several years and, in fact, were part of a close-knit group of guys called "the brotherhood." That morning, Matt asked if I would run him to the doctor's office. He'd had a nagging cough for several weeks and wanted to get some medicine to shake it.

Neither of us had any idea that that visit to the doctor would lead to a series of tests and x-rays that would eventually diagnose Matt as having a form of cancer known as Hodgkins disease. The whole college rallied around Matt. He eventually had to go home to Virginia to get the medical treatment and attention he needed. We were all thrilled when Matt arrived back on campus the next semester, full

...the hope that endures for all times

from the album
FACE THE
NATION

Why?

They say that into every life some
    rain must fall
For the pain is no respecter of the
    mighty or the small
But sometimes it just seems so
    unfair
To see the One who's had more
    than His share
Oh it makes you wonder why
And Lord I wouldn't second guess
Your mighty plan
For I know You have a purpose
    that's beyond the scope of man
If You look inside my heart You will
    find
That I have always been the
    trusting kind
Oh but still I wonder

(Chorus)
Why do the rainy days have to
    come
When the storm clouds hide the
    sun
I wanna know why

of life and with no trace of cancer
in his body. Since we were both
ministry majors, we got part-time
jobs at a local church. He worked
as youth pastor, I worked as the
minister of music, and we had the
time of our lives.

In 1986, I graduated Lee and
went on the road singing contemporary Christian music. Matt
eventually became a youth pastor at one of the cornerstone
churches in the denomination we
had both grown up in.

One day on the road, I
received an urgent phone call
from one of my college buddies:
"Matt has leukemia." I was
shocked. Matt battled leukemia
and eventually went into remis-
sion. Once again Matt overcame
a life-threatening disease.

Several years passed, and once
again I received another phone
call with a message about Matt:
his leukemia was out of remis-
sion. For many months Matt battled the disease, and at the end of
1993, he exited this world and
went home to a place that he'd
sung, talked, and preached about
many times throughout his life.

During the ten years Matt battled the cancer and leukemia, none of us believed the end result would be death. Because of our faith in God, we felt certain that Matt would be healed and would live to be a testimony of God's miraculous power. But it didn't happen that way. And we wondered why.

We still wonder why.

A strong, young Christian couple prays for a baby only to have the life of that innocent child taken in a drive-by shooting—and they wonder *why?* . . . A Christian husband sits at a table and stares off into oblivion because his wife has just come in and told him she doesn't want to be married anymore. And he wonders *why?*. . . . A fifty-five year old man has given his life to his company only to be told he is no longer needed. He can't help but ask *why?*. . . A loving mother dies leaving two pre-teen daughters without a mom. They now must face the complexities of being a teen without their mother there. They look up to the heavens and ask *why?*

Why? We scramble and shuffle through our human reasoning, searching for a neat, clean answer. Why? We grow insecure because the God in whom we have placed all of our faith seems to have let us all down. Why? We struggle to see how "all things work together for the good," and our hearts scream *why?*

Why? Why? Why? That's exactly what I thought as I stood in the cemetery that December afternoon staring at the grave of my friend.

It has been several years since Matt went home to be with the Lord. Because Matt was such an inspiration to so many of us who knew him, he is still missed. Although I still wonder why, I have finally accepted the fact that I

175

...the hope that endures for all times

Why when the reasons aren't clear
    to me
When it all is a mystery
I want to know why
And though down here I may not
    understand
I won't let go of the Unseen Hand
For It holds the reasons why

The Lord has never been afraid of
    honest prayers
And He won't allow the burden to
    be more than you can bear
When He knows that your trust is
    in Him
He doesn't mind the questions now
    and then
Even if you wonder

don't have to understand everything.

But I do understand that God
has called us to trust him, regard-
less of the circumstances. I do
understand that God is at
work—always. And I do understand that when I don't know the
answer to *why*, I do know the
answer to *who*. And that answer
is God!

When life is simple, I will hold
to his hand. When life is complicated, I will hold to his hand. And
someday, I will do more than
hold his hand; I will leave this
world to be with him, as Matt did
that dark December day.

Questions to Ponder

1. What in life has caused you to ask *why?*
2. How do you handle your unanswered questions? Do you resent God? Are you angry? Confused?
3. Where are you on your pathway to learning to trust God when you don't understand why?

Back to the Basics

Take your negative emotions and doubts to God, lay them at his feet, and tell him how you feel. Be honest. God can take it. Then ask him to replace your doubts with trust. Knowing that God can create something from nothing, believe that he can create trust in you where there is none.

After the hurt is gone

No matter what you do, life goes on.

4HIM

STDX-007013

BENSON

COMPAC
DIGITAL AUDIO

and

e For You

s Faith

Bread Of Life

On

I Am Gone

Produced by Don Koch
Produced by Jonathan David Brown
Produced by Chris Harris and
Mark Heimermann for
Funattic Productions

Even when I am afraid, I keep on trusting you.

Psalm 56:3 *CEV*

Life Goes On

Andy Chrisman

I hate turbulence. As I write, I'm headed for Phoenix on a DC–9 that is experiencing the clear-air variety somewhere over New Mexico. Now, I understand that a little choppy air doesn't mean that our plane will soon be plummeting to the earth in flames. However, sometimes these nondestructive bumps and drops can send even the most seasoned traveler reaching for the airsick bag. Maybe I've seen too many air-disaster movies. Perhaps it's because my wife, Jackie, used to be a flight attendant and was injured more than once due to heavy turbulence. Could it be that my lack of control over the situation makes me jumpy every time the big hunk of flying metal dips and dives? (It still hasn't smoothed out, by the way.) Whatever the reason, I hate it! Can't the pilot divert us to some

...the hope that endures for all times

from the album
4 H I M

Life Goes On

In every life there will come a time
When the weight of the world
    crashes around you
Everyone says it will be just fine
But they really don't know all that
    you've been through
Trying hard to get through the
    struggle
Knowing that tomorrow you'll find

(Chorus)
This isn't all there is
Life goes on (Goes on)
There's so much more than this
Life goes on (Goes on)
So don't let the moment deceive
    you
'Cause after the hurt is gone
No matter what you do
Life goes on

When you are facing your darkest
    night
Just remember the race isn't quite
    over

calmer air, like maybe over Kansas? Must we stick to our predestined flight plan?

The parallels to life are obvious. We buckle up and casually head toward our destination. The air is smooth, the seats are comfy, and then wham!—bump city. How many times have things been running smoothly in your life when the bottom completely dropped out? Why does it seem we always have to go through some turbulence to get to our "Phoenix"? Is there life after failure, after heartache, after disaster?

The disciples didn't think so. They locked themselves in a room after Jesus was crucified, scared to death that they would be next. One day they were walking comfortably alongside the Messiah, the next they were cowering behind closed doors, their lives seemingly over. "How will we ever face our families?" they must have thought. "Who will hire us now? How will we make a living? Will we ever be able to trust in anything again?" How fatal their thoughts must have

180

been: "It's over; we're finished." And it was just about then that Jesus came waltzing through the front door. "Why are you so frightened?" He asked. And by the way, "Do you have something to eat?" (Luke 24:38, 41).

Just when you think your life is over, God walks through the front door and says, "It ain't over till I say it's over. And by the way, I'm hungry!" God has a way of putting things into perspective. Your problems are no big deal to him. If he can create the entire universe, surely he can get you through your turbulent times. Your trials are just choppy air to the Pilot. This plane isn't going down; it's going to Phoenix. And no setback is going to keep it from getting there.

Life goes on. It may not seem possible at times, but it does move ahead. One day, when we *really are* at the end of our lives, we'll have the luxury of looking back and seeing just how well orchestrated our journey was. There were no wrong turns, no missed connections. It's just that sometimes you have to hike through the desert to get to the ocean or climb a rugged mountain to get to the green valley or change planes in LA to get to Hawaii. It's all part of the itinerary on a journey whose destination is the Gates of Glory. What's sixty, seventy, eighty years of turbulence compared to an eternity in paradise?

Ah, the sweet screech of tires touching the runway and the roar of engines in full reversal thrust. What a ride! (Funny I didn't feel that way five paragraphs ago!) Remember, the hard times won't last forever, so hang in there (Romans 5:3–5). Knowing your eventual destination, you'll want to stay on board, your seat belt securely fastened, your seat back all the way forward, and your tray table in its upright and locked position . . .

. . . the hope that endures for all times

Jesus has promised eternal life
And the ones who believe soon will
   discover
This is not the end of the story
This is not the end of the line

(Chorus)

Questions to Ponder

1. Are you experiencing any turbulence in your life right now? What is it?
2. When you look back at past turbulences in your life, can you now see God's hand in the journey? How did he work?
3. How has God reassured you in the past? How can you rely on those reassurances to help you through the present?

Back to the Basics

Trusting God doesn't calm the turbulence, but it will soothe your heart. It won't smooth the ride, but it will steady your soul. Trust has a supernatural power to squelch the anxieties that torment your mind. The next time your world starts shaking, lift your eyes to the heavens and focus on the one who is in control of it all: "Fix your eyes on Jesus, the author and perfector of your faith" (Hebrews 12:2 NIV).

...the hope that endures for all times

You are the reason I can't deny the truth
I can't get past the evidence of You

> What can we say about all this? If God is on our side, can anyone be against us? God did not keep back his own Son, but he gave him for us. If God did this, won't he freely give us everything else?
>
> Romans 8:31–32 *CEV*

Can't Get Past the Evidence

Mark Harris

Simon Peter had become quite the preacher. He was the most passionate orator of the whole gang. He was bold and forthright, unafraid to stand before a crowd and talk about Jesus the Savior.

That is, until the night when his whole world collapsed. The Messiah, who'd promised to bring him and the other disciples into his kingdom, had been arrested, shamefully bound, and had stood meekly before the high priest, calmly answering his incessant questions. After a reckless display of bravery in the Garden where they arrested Jesus, Peter had followed the mob that led Jesus away. But when he stood outside the high priest's courtyard, his bravery deserted him. His passion waned. When asked if he were

...the hope that endures for all times

from the album
O B V I O U S

Can't Get Past the Evidence

You broke into this world of mine
Stole my heart you robbed me blind
While I wasn't looking at all
Without a warning or a sign
It seems you caught me by surprise
Now I know the reason why
Love is the alibi

(Chorus 1)
And I can't get past the evidence
I can't get past the proof
I can't get past the evidence
It's impossible to do
I can't get past the evidence
And I can't deny the truth
I can't get past the evidence of You

We look for pieces on the way
To fit the puzzles of this place
Is there an equation to life
But in the midst of every day
There is a clue there is a trace

one of Jesus' disciples, Peter denied even knowing him . . . he denied it three times.

And then the shame had come. The remorse. He'd always been the one to stand up and be brave—but not this time. This time he had totally humiliated himself. This time he had denied his Lord. He didn't know if Jesus would ever forgive him.

And now, here he was face-to-face with the one he had let down, all alone, just him and Jesus. Perhaps he expected Jesus to lambaste him, to chastise him for his weakness, but he didn't. Instead, Jesus looked through Peter's eyes into his very soul and asked one, pointed question: "Simon Peter, do you love me?"

Peter's answer was quick and sure, "Yes, Lord, you know that I love you."

"Then feed my lambs," Jesus said.

Three times, Jesus asked Peter the same question, three times Peter said yes, and three times Jesus told him to feed his sheep. What was the significance of this line of questioning? Some have

186

pointed out that the Greek word for *love* that Jesus used the first two times was a stronger word than Peter used, suggesting that Jesus wanted a higher intensity love from Peter than Peter was at that time willing to give. Was there any correlation between Peter's three denials on the night of Jesus' crucifixion and Jesus' three requests for his love? Was Jesus trying to refocus Peter on his mission after his failure in the courtyard?

Whatever the significance, we see that Jesus was asking for a commitment from Peter—but not a commitment of accomplishments, not a promise to do more, preach better, fight more bravely. No, Jesus was asking for a commitment of love—love for him and thus love for his sheep.

For much of my life, I personally tried to prove my love for God through accomplishments. I felt as if God required me to earn his approval through singing, preaching, and constantly laboring for his cause. But a few years ago, I suddenly realized that God wasn't looking to be impressed by my works and talents; God simply wanted me to grow in my love for him and to be a witness of his overwhelming love to his sheep.

Notice that Jesus didn't have to tell Peter that he loved him. Jesus had demonstrated that love just a few days before as he gave his life on the Cross. Although Peter must have felt much shame at what he'd done, he couldn't get past the evidence of Christ's love for him. That evidence is there for us too. Jesus' love for us isn't based on what we do or how well we do it. All he asks of us is that we love him and that we feed his sheep as we share the witness of his love with others.

When I finally heard Jesus say to me, "Mark, do you love me?" I understand that Jesus wasn't asking me to prove

...the hope that endures for all times

A remnant of love remains
I'm ready to rest my case

(Chorus 2)
And I can't get past the evidence
I can't get past the proof
I can't get past the evidence
It's impossible to do
You are the reason that I can't
    deny the truth
I can't get past the evidence of You

(Bridge)
Beyond the shadow of a doubt I
    see the light
I'm a victim of a love I can't deny
I'll be the first to testify, that
I can't get past the evidence of You

(Chorus)

my love through accomplishments; he was refocusing my
heart on the value of simply loving him. And as he asked for a
confirmation of my love, the evidence of his love for me flooded
my heart. I was convicted that his
love was pursuing me, admon-
ishing me: "Stand still long
enough to experience my love;
stop laboring! Love me, and let
me love you!" I have learned that
anything I do publicly for Christ
is simply an overflow of my relationship of love with him. If my
labor for him replaces my time
with him, then my priorities are
out of order.

God longs to meet us in quiet
places. There his love overwhelms us and our hearts
respond in kind. Once we are
alone with him, we can't deny
the truth and we can't deny the
evidence that he loves us and
that he is a rewarder of those
who diligently seek him. Maybe
it's been a while since you've
stood still long enough to hear
God speaking to you. Perhaps
you've been trying to avoid the

confrontation because you've been relying on accomplishments to earn his love.

Stand still for a moment and listen. Let God overwhelm you like he did Peter that day on the shore, like he did me a few years back and is still doing today. Let him overwhelm you with the evidence of his love.

Questions to Ponder

1. Have you ever failed Jesus like Peter did? How did you feel?
2. Have you allowed Jesus to reassure you of his love for you? How have you responded to his request for a commitment of love from you?
3. Who are Jesus' sheep today? How can you feed them?
4. Have you tried to prove your love for Jesus by your accomplishments? What does he want you to do instead?

Back to the Basics

Meet God in a quiet place today. No matter how busy you are, no matter how stressed, take a few minutes to be alone with him. Open your heart to being washed with his love. Allow him to fill your heart to the point of overflowing so you will have love to share with his sheep.

...the hope that endures for all times

'Cause it's not in the grave for the skeptics to see
But He lives in the hearts of the ones who believe

4 Him

The message

BENSON

Don't you know? Haven't you heard? The Lord
is the eternal God, Creator of the earth.

Isaiah 40:28 *CEV*

All the Evidence
I Need

Kirk Sullivan

Do you ever question God's existence? Do you ever wonder if he hears your prayers or if he cares at all? Even Christians sometimes have doubts. But our loving God has provided us with all the evidence we need that he is and that he cares.

If it's physical, scientific evidence that we need—there is plenty. Josh McDowell, in his classic book *Evidence that Demands a Verdict*, presents amazing physical, scientific evidence that God is. And recently, I watched a series of tapes my parents told me about called *Creation in Symphony*. I was amazed at the abundance of physical evidence that supports the biblical account of creation. These tapes changed the way I view the Word of God and have greatly increased my faith. In addition to the ones I've

...the hope that endures for all times

from the album
THE MESSAGE

All the Evidence I Need

Well I've seen the news and I've
heard the questions
Seems the thing to do is to keep
second guessing
The One who made the earth and
sky
I guess it's okay just to wonder why
But I know the truth, and I know I'm
certain
It's not a mystery, it's not behind a
curtain
The veil was torn many years ago
And the Spirit stayed just to let us
know
That the answer is not in the stars
way up high
But the answer is found in believing
in Christ

(Chorus)
So I am walking by faith and not by
sight
And I am trusting in invisible things
For I have felt in my heart what I
can't
See with my eyes 'cause the proof
is living
Inside of me, I've been set free,
and

mentioned, there are many books and videos that are excellent resources to increase the faith of Christians and to bring non-believers to a faith in God.

Besides the scientific, physical evidence, the fingerprints of God's goodness are everywhere. Countless hospitals, orphan homes, and relief organizations have been built because compassionate Christians have followed the example of Christ in reaching out to the sick, the weak, and the hurting of this world. When disaster strikes, it is not the atheistic organizations of the world that respond with food, blankets, hugs, and help; it is Christian people who are moved to compassion because they follow a compassionate Lord.

But the most compelling evidence to me is the evidence of changed lives. I've seen the very nature of a person change in midlife. I've seen men consumed by anger and violence become peace-loving husbands and fathers who care for and cherish their families. I've seen the emotional wounds of abuse healed, and I've seen hope restored to the hopeless. I've seen marriages mended; I've seen people delivered from alcohol and drugs. I've seen physical healing come to my friend Marty Magehee.

And then there's me. Every morning when I look into the mirror, I see the face of a man changed by God. Even though God's love is intangible, I know it's there because it has changed my very nature. He renews my mind through his Word; he gives me peace when circumstances dictate chaos; he gifts me with wisdom, strength, and a sound mind. I know it is God who is at work in me because I have no ability to change myself.

And what about you? Has God worked in your life to bring about changes that you were totally incapable of making. When you look over your shoulder at your past, do you see evidence of God's tender hand on your life when you needed comfort? Has he cleansed you from sin? Has he lifted the load of guilt from your heart? Has he purged you of anger; has he calmed your fears? The evidence is right there—staring back at you in the mirror. You may have to take an archaeological dig into your heart to unearth the evidence there, but if you'll dig deeply, you will discover a mound of evidence in your own back yard of history.

While I value the scientific evidence that confirms God's Word, my faith is not built on the latest archaeological finds, my faith is built on the evidence of his goodness in our world and on his power to change and heal lives. That's all the evidence I need!

...the hope that endures for all times

This is all the evidence I need

There are pyramids in the land of
  Egypt
And there are those who say that
  they contain the secrets
To where we're from and why
  we're here
But I think God's Word makes it
  crystal clear
That the ancient tombs in the bar-
  ren desert
Do not hold the clues, they do not
  hold the answers
The truth has already been
  revealed
For it's moving in me and I know
  it's real
'Cause it's not in the grave for the
  skeptics to see
But He lives in the hearts of the
  ones who believe

(Chorus)

(Bridge)
'Cause I know Your love reaches
  out
To me in my weakest of days
For I've felt Your touch
In my heart of hearts
Though I've never even seen Your
  face

All the Evidence I Need by Mark Harris, Keith Dudley,
and Don Koch © 1996 Paragon Music Corp./Point
Clear Music/ASCAP/Acuff-Rose Music, Inc./Defini-
tive Music (admin. by Word, Inc.)/Dayspring Music (a
div. of Word, Inc.)/BMI. All rights reserved. Used by
permsiion.

Questions to Ponder

1. Have you had periods of
   doubt in your life? How
   have you handled that
   doubt? Where are you now
   in your belief?
2. What physical evidence in
   the world increases your
   conviction that God exists?
3. What evidence of God's
   goodness do you see in the
   world around you?
4. What changes has God
   brought about in you that
   you know you could not
   have done on your own?

Back to the Basics

There's not much that is more
basic than our belief in God. If you
have lingering doubts, don't be
afraid to look for answers. Truth
does not fear investigation. But
don't just ask the questions and let
it go at that. Seek answers. Read;
ask people you trust for guidance;
pray. Bring any lingering doubts to
God. Pray the prayer of the father
of the demon possessed boy: "I do
have faith! Please help me to have
even more" (Mark 9:24).

194

...the hope that endures for all times

Oh to face the jungle of impossibilities and have no doubt

To trust what I can't see and know the lion that's in me will lead me out

> But those who trust the Lord will find new strength.
> They will be strong like eagles soaring upward on
> wings; they will walk and run without getting tired.

Isaiah 40:31 CEV

Let the Lion Run Free

Andy Chrisman

Potential. How many times have you heard that word in reference to you? "You have great potential." For me it has always been a daunting reminder that the bar of excellence and achievement has been set high by my family and friends. "You have great potential." I remember the day my mom nudged me on stage when I was seven years old to sing one of Bill and Gloria Gaither's songs:

> I am a promise.
> I am a possibility.
> I am a promise with a capital P.
> I am a great big bundle of potentiality.

Parents always have high hopes for their children (I'm convinced my son will be president one day), but do we

...the hope that endures for all times

from the album
O B V I O U S

Let the Lion Run Free

I can dream the dream the dreamer
    lives inside of me
It's just that way
I can only reach what I believe
    'cause I can't reach
Beyond my faith
No, I'm no limited by what has
    always been
It's time to break this status quo
    and take a leap and
Jump out of my skin

(Chorus)
Break these chains, open this cage
Let the lion run free
destiny awaits, beyond these gates
Let the lion run free
Let the lion run free

Oh to face the jungle of
    impossibilities and have no doubt
To trust what I can't see and know
    the lion that's in me
Will lead me out
I'll take the challenge go into the
    great unknown

honestly have a clue about what our heavenly Father expects from us? "You have great potential," he whispers to our hearts. Sometimes, though, it's difficult to look past our shortcomings to see the promise of greatness that lies within.

Perhaps we'd get a better perspective if we'd take a look at our blueprints. As architectural achievements go, our human design is the Frank Lloyd Wright of all creations, a construction of monumental and unprecedented proportions.

- Consider the mind, thought by scientists to be the greatest supercomputer ever assembled (and we only use a fraction of its capabilities).
- Or how about the heart? It has the capacity to love, let go, forgive, reject, choose, follow a whim, follow a cause, or follow a devotion.
- And what of the spirit?— capable of winning or losing with class, competent to set a goal and see it through

to completion, able to take an unfair situation and triumph over it, strong enough to persevere against all odds and never give up.

• And don't forget about the soul. Its eternal nature and expandability enable it to house the Creator of the universe.

What a shame that we keep all that incredible potential bottled up for most of our lives.

Every time I take my children to the zoo, I can't help but feel sorry for those caged-up animals. The exotic birds can fly only as high as the tops of their cages; the snakes can only slither as far as their Plexi-glass walls. There's no way to truly appreciate these beautiful creatures outside their natural habitat. It's sad to see them trapped within unnatural boundaries in a world that stifles their instincts.

And what about those lions, the kings of the jungle? They should be out ruling the savanna, stalking their prey, orchestrating the natural order of their society. Instead, there they lay, dozing in the sun, tuning out my kids who are begging for their attention. It's as if they've grown accustomed to their bondage. There's no way out, so there's no use dreaming of what could have been.

And what about the lion that lives within each of us? Is he bound and caged? Is he ten thousand miles from where he is destined to be? What about all that potential that everyone has always said you have? Is it lazing on a rock in the sun, sleeping as the world goes by? It's time to break the chains, open the cage, and let the lion run free. It's time to live up to the potential that God created in you—the ability to change the world, the power to change yourself. Once you've tapped into that well of possibilities, you'll

...the hope that endures for all times

It's time to wake this giant that's in
me, let my inhibitions go

(Chorus)

soon realize there's no end to it. It is infinite!

The one scripture that blows my mind more than any other verse in the Bible is John 14:12. Jesus proclaims, "I tell you for certain that if you have faith in me, you will do the same things that I am doing. You will do even greater things, now that I am going back to the Father." Can you believe that! All of Christ's power is right there, right there in your mind, your heart, your spirit, your soul. Deity has taken up residency inside of you! You have the mind of Christ, the heart of God, the indwelling of the Holy Spirit, and an immortal soul—all wrapped up in a rather attractive suit of epidermis. Sounds like Superman to me.

You know what your potential is. You've probably always known it. But you've allowed doubt and self-pity to chain it up for so long that your prison feels like home. Remember that home is where your heart is, and in your heart, dreams never die. God has invested himself in you. Don't shortchange him. Unleash the lion run he has placed within you; let him run free in the jungle of possibilities.

Now get going—your destiny awaits.

Questions to Ponder

1. What potential, what promise, lies within you that is not fully tapped?
2. How does it make you feel to realize that God actually lives inside of you?
3. What barriers keep you from allowing your lion to run free?

Back to the Basics

God has put abilities and potential within you, and he has placed them there for one purpose only: to bring glory to him. Your life, lived to its fullest, is a testimony to the power and love of God. Take your gifts and your inhibitions and lay them at the feet of your Father. Ask him to help you break down the walls of fear that inhibit you; ask him to help you become the child of promise he created you to be.

Epilogue

For years we have been privileged to minister in song. Now you have participated in our ministry through the written word. It is our prayer that this book has been a genuine blessing to you. The ultimate power to change comes from God, and we hope you have been drawn closer to him by the devotionals you have read. And as you are drawn closer to God, may you be inspired to live 4 Him.

Because of the Savior,